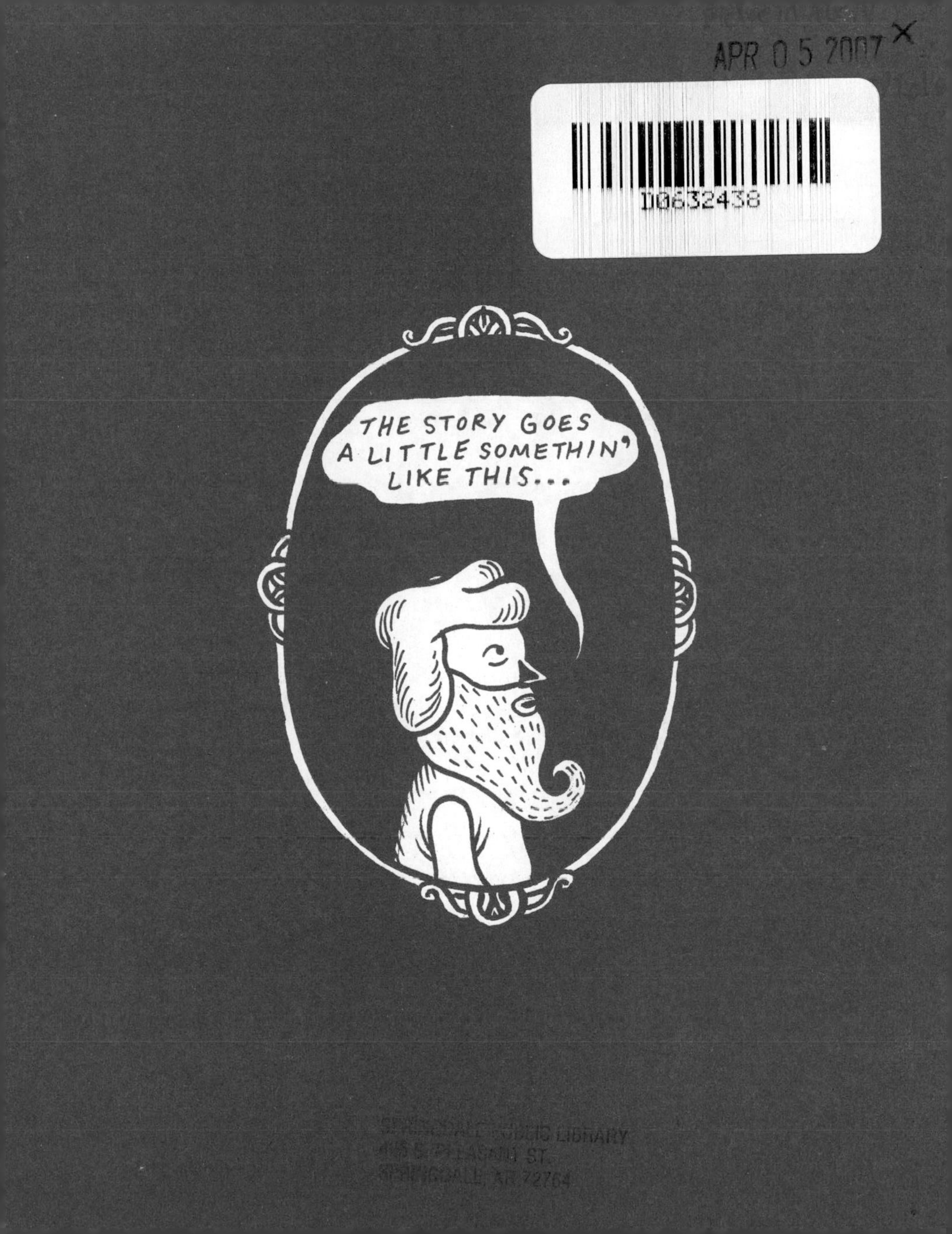
THE STORY GOES A LITTLE SOMETHIN' LIKE THIS...

ISBN 1-891830-84-8
1. Folk Tales
2. Cartoons
3. Graphic Novels

Tales of Woodsman Pete © 2006 Lille Carrè. Published by
Top Shelf Productions, PO Box 1282, Marietta, GA 30061-
1282, USA. Publishers: Brett Warnock and Chris Staros. Top
Shelf Productions® and the Top Shelf logo are registered
trademarks of Top Shelf Productions, Inc. All Rights Reserved.
No part of this publication may be reproduced without
permission, except for small excerpts for purposes of review.
Visit our online catalog at www.topshelfcomix.com. First
Printing, May 2006. Printed in Canada.

TALES OF WOODSMAN PETE

WITH FULL PARTICULARS

BY LILLI CARRÉ

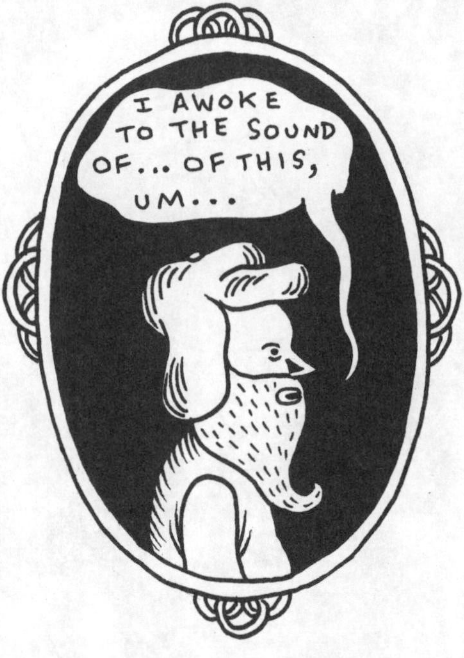
I AWOKE TO THE SOUND OF... OF THIS, UM...

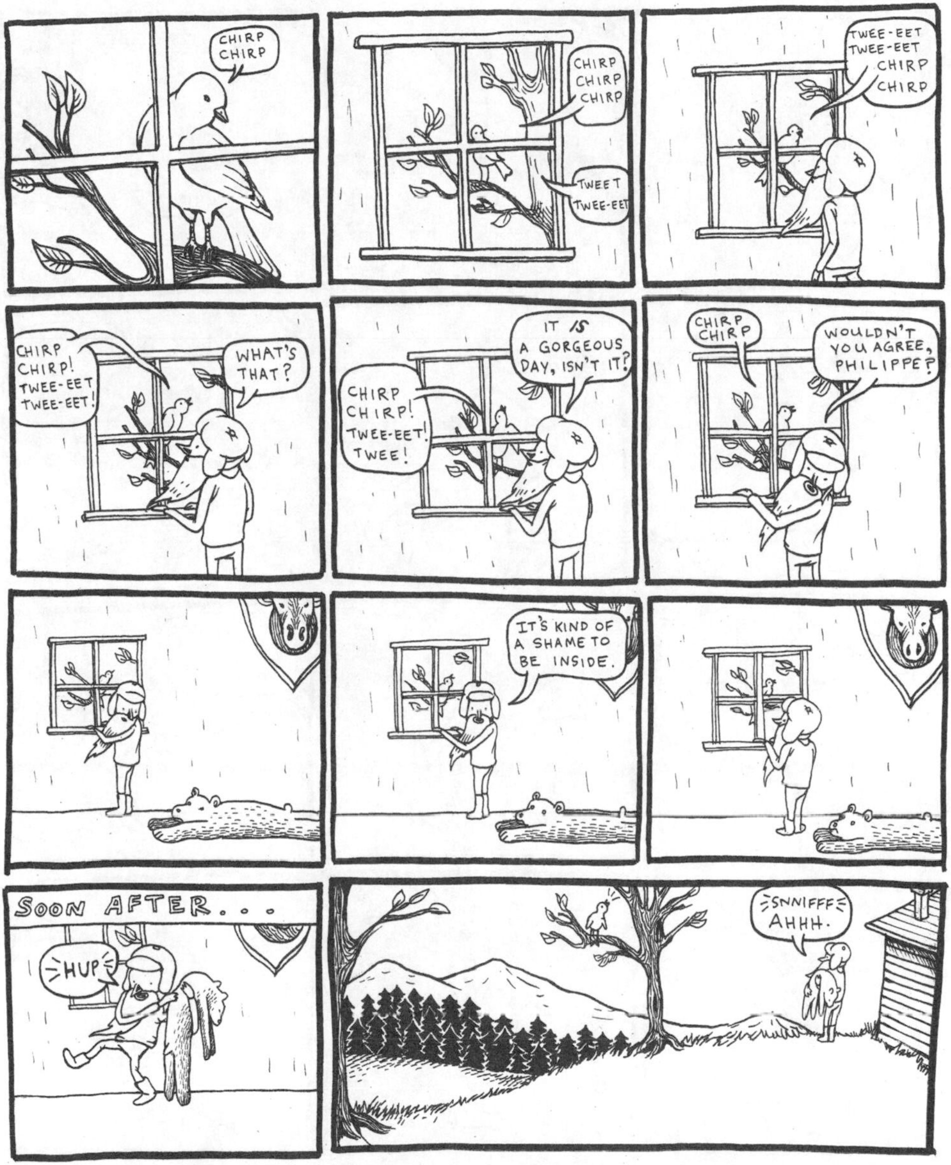
CHIRP CHIRP
CHIRP CHIRP CHIRP
TWEET TWEE-EET
TWEE-EET TWEE-EET CHIRP CHIRP
CHIRP CHIRP! TWEE-EET TWEE-EET!
WHAT'S THAT?
CHIRP CHIRP! TWEE-EET! TWEE!
IT *IS* A GORGEOUS DAY, ISN'T IT?
CHIRP CHIRP
WOULDN'T YOU AGREE, PHILIPPE?
IT'S KIND OF A SHAME TO BE INSIDE.
SOON AFTER...
HUP
SNNIFFF AHHH.

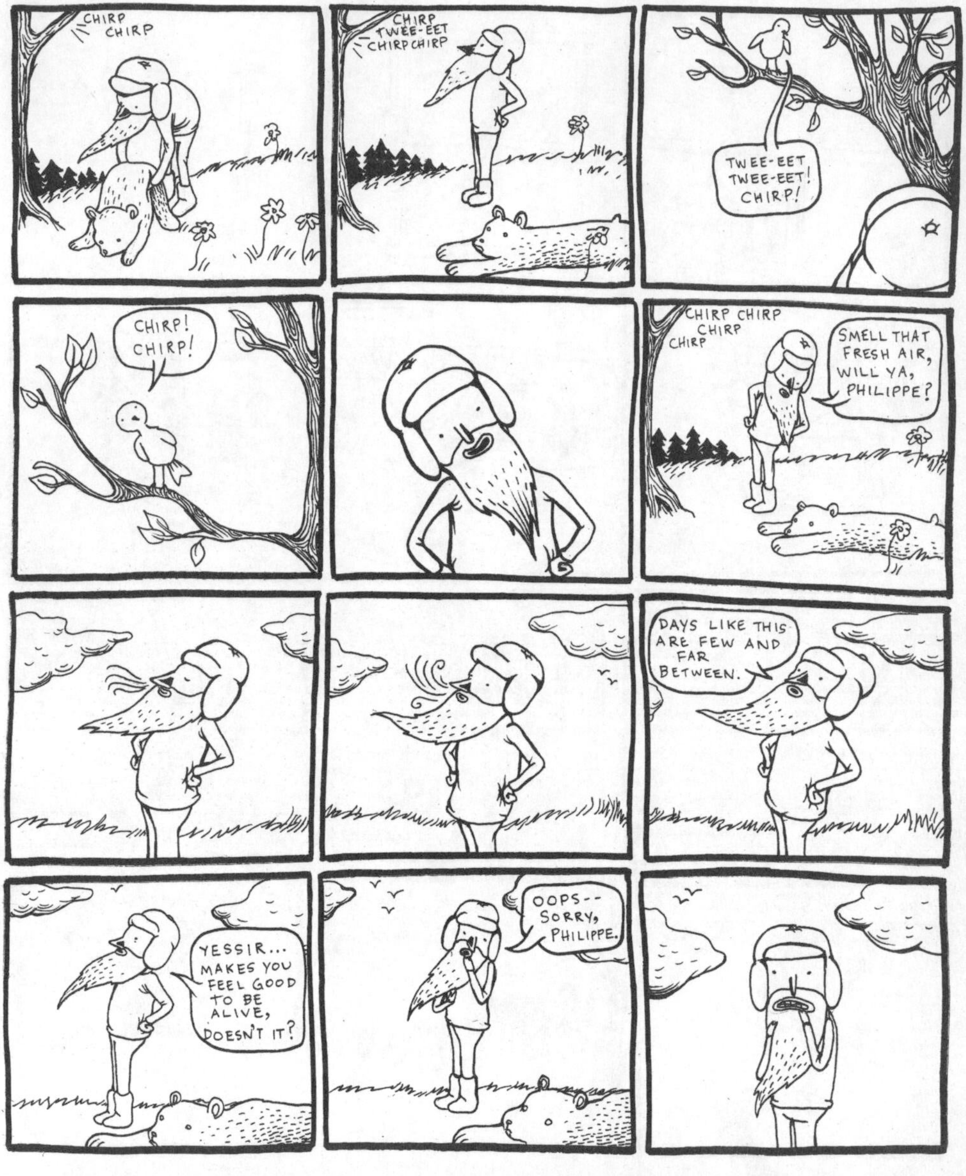
CHIRP
CHIRP
CHIRP
TWEE-EET
CHIRP CHIRP
TWEE-EET TWEE-EET! CHIRP!
CHIRP! CHIRP!
CHIRP CHIRP
CHIRP
CHIRP
SMELL THAT FRESH AIR, WILL YA, PHILIPPE?
DAYS LIKE THIS ARE FEW AND FAR BETWEEN.
YESSIR... MAKES YOU FEEL GOOD TO BE ALIVE, DOESN'T IT?
OOPS-- SORRY, PHILIPPE.

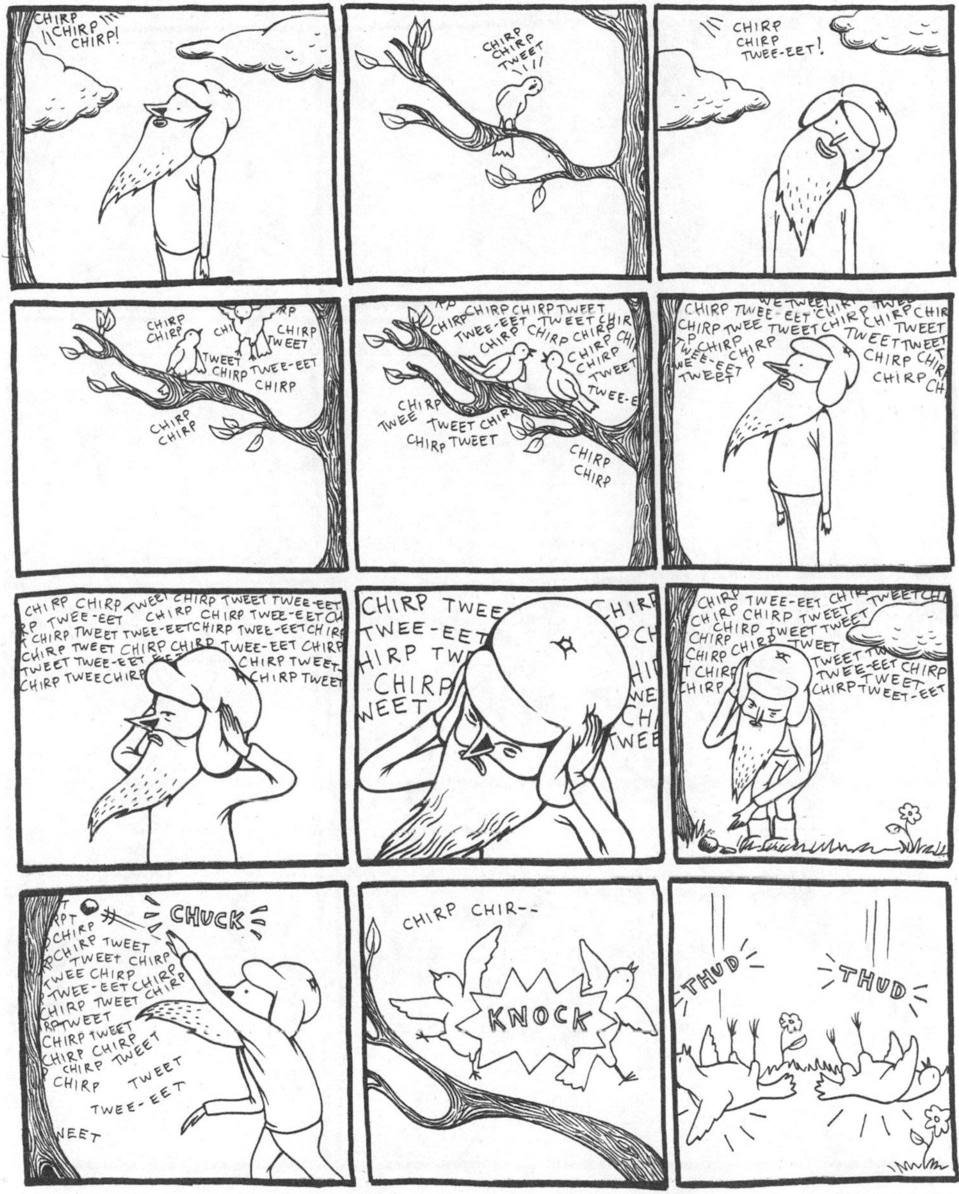
CHIRP CHIRP CHIRP!
CHIRP CHIRP TWEET
CHIRP CHIRP TWEE-EET!
CHIRP CHIRP
CHIRP TWEET
TWEET CHIRP TWEE-EET CHIRP
CHIRP CHIRP
CHIRP CHIRP TWEET TWEE-EET TWEET
CHIRP CHIRP CHIRP
TWEE TWEET CHIRP CHIRP TWEET
CHIRP CHIRP
CHIRP TWEE-EET TWEET CHIRP
CHIRP TWEE TWEET CHIRP TWEET
TWEET TWEET CHIRP
CHIRP CHIRP TWEET CHIRP TWEET TWEE-EET
CHIRP TWEE-EET CHIRP CHIRP TWEE-EET
CHIRP TWEET TWEE-EET CHIRP TWEE-EET
CHIRP TWEET CHIRP CHIRP TWEE-EET CHIRP
CHIRP TWEE-EET
CHIRP TWEE-EET
CHIRP TWEET
CHIRP TWEE-EET TWEET
CHIRP CHIRP TWEET TWEET
TWEE-EET CHIRP
CHIRP TWEET TWEET-EET
CHUCK
CHIRP TWEET
TWEE CHIRP
TWEE-EET CHIRP
CHIRP TWEET CHIRP
CHIRP TWEET
CHIRP CHIRP TWEET
CHIRP TWEET
TWEE-EET
CHIRP CHIR--
KNOCK
THUD
THUD

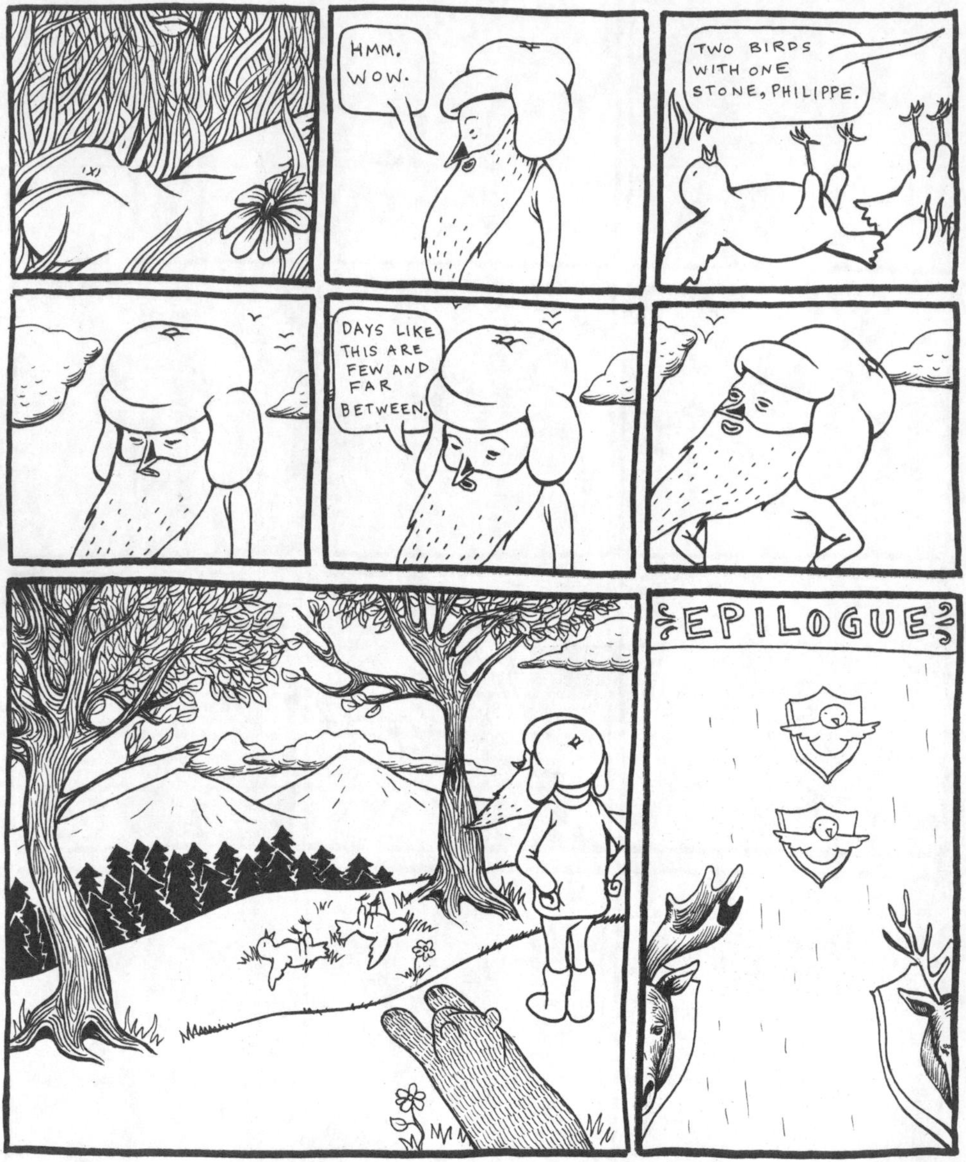
HMM. WOW.
TWO BIRDS WITH ONE STONE, PHILIPPE.
DAYS LIKE THIS ARE FEW AND FAR BETWEEN.
EPILOGUE

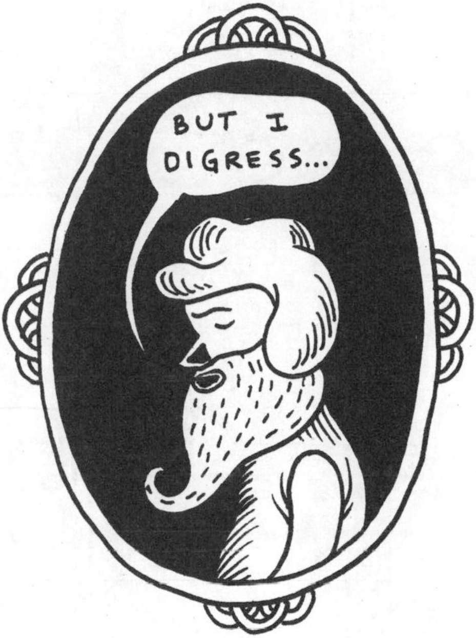
BUT I DIGRESS...

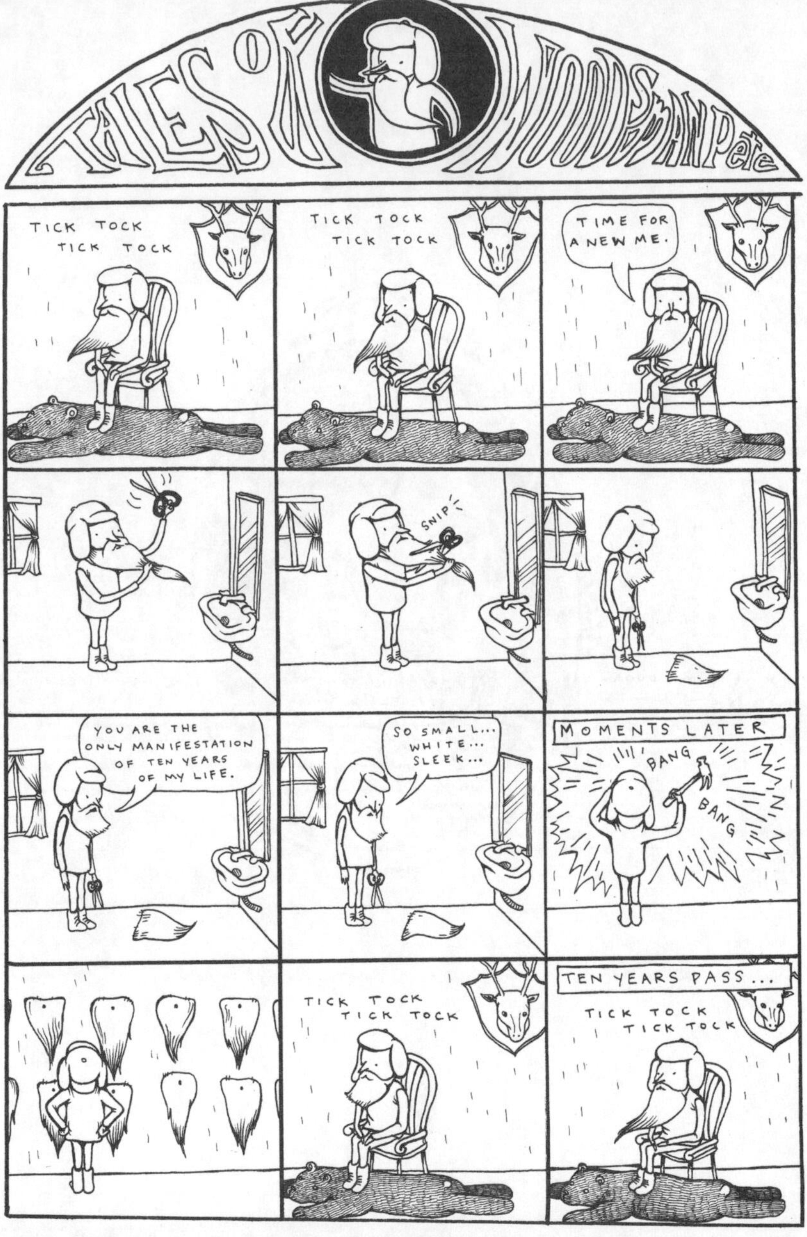
TALES OF WOODSMAN PETE
TICK TOCK
TICK TOCK
TICK TOCK
TICK TOCK
TIME FOR A NEW ME.
SNIP
YOU ARE THE ONLY MANIFESTATION OF TEN YEARS OF MY LIFE.
SO SMALL... WHITE... SLEEK...
MOMENTS LATER
BANG
BANG
BANG
TICK TOCK
TICK TOCK
TEN YEARS PASS...
TICK TOCK
TICK TOCK

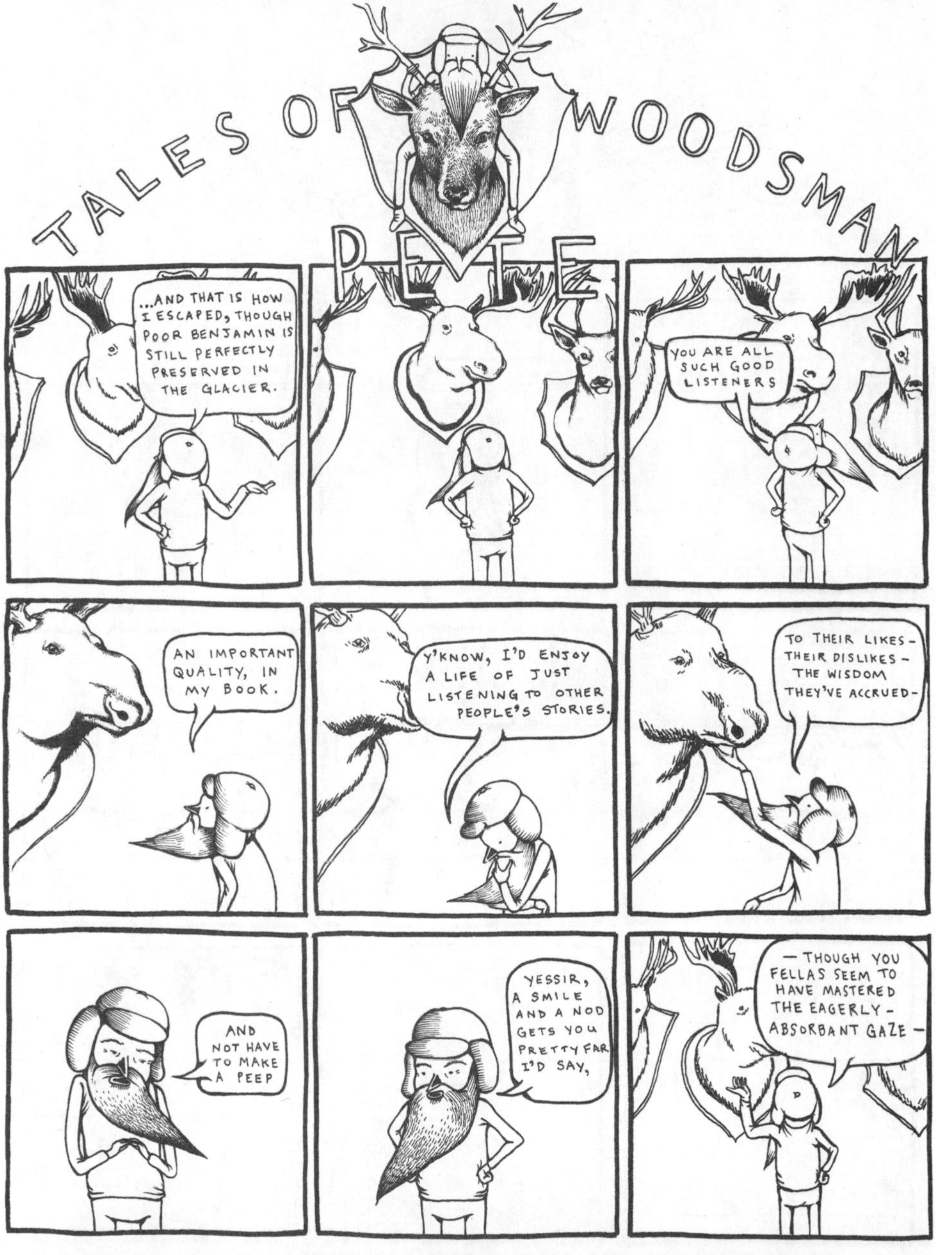
TALES OF WOODSMAN PETE
...AND THAT IS HOW I ESCAPED, THOUGH POOR BENJAMIN IS STILL PERFECTLY PRESERVED IN THE GLACIER.
YOU ARE ALL SUCH GOOD LISTENERS
AN IMPORTANT QUALITY, IN MY BOOK.
Y'KNOW, I'D ENJOY A LIFE OF JUST LISTENING TO OTHER PEOPLE'S STORIES.
TO THEIR LIKES - THEIR DISLIKES - THE WISDOM THEY'VE ACCRUED-
AND NOT HAVE TO MAKE A PEEP
YESSIR, A SMILE AND A NOD GETS YOU PRETTY FAR I'D SAY,
— THOUGH YOU FELLAS SEEM TO HAVE MASTERED THE EAGERLY-ABSORBANT GAZE —

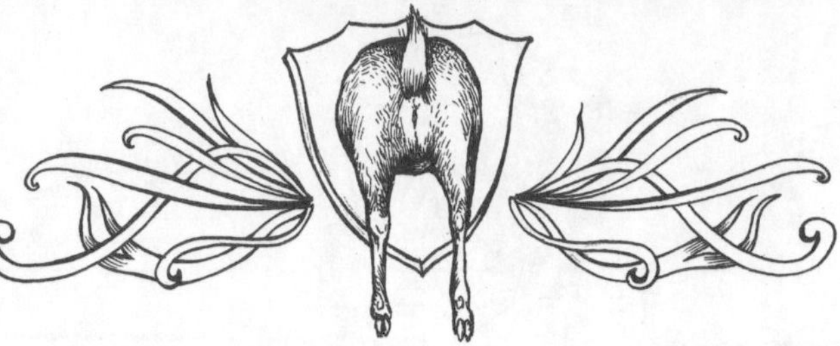

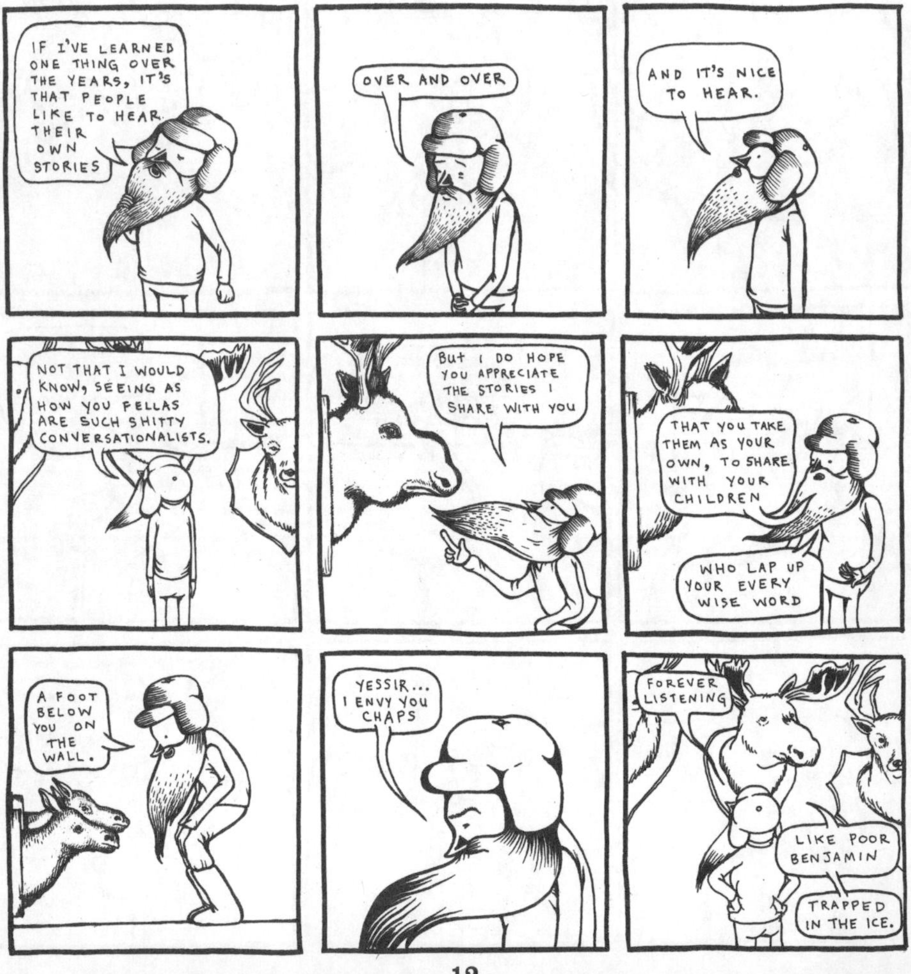
IF I'VE LEARNED ONE THING OVER THE YEARS, IT'S THAT PEOPLE LIKE TO HEAR THEIR OWN STORIES
OVER AND OVER
AND IT'S NICE TO HEAR.
NOT THAT I WOULD KNOW, SEEING AS HOW YOU FELLAS ARE SUCH SHITTY CONVERSATIONALISTS.
But I DO HOPE YOU APPRECIATE THE STORIES I SHARE WITH YOU
THAT YOU TAKE THEM AS YOUR OWN, TO SHARE WITH YOUR CHILDREN
WHO LAP UP YOUR EVERY WISE WORD
A FOOT BELOW YOU ON THE WALL.
YESSIR... I ENVY YOU CHAPS
FOREVER LISTENING
LIKE POOR BENJAMIN
TRAPPED IN THE ICE.

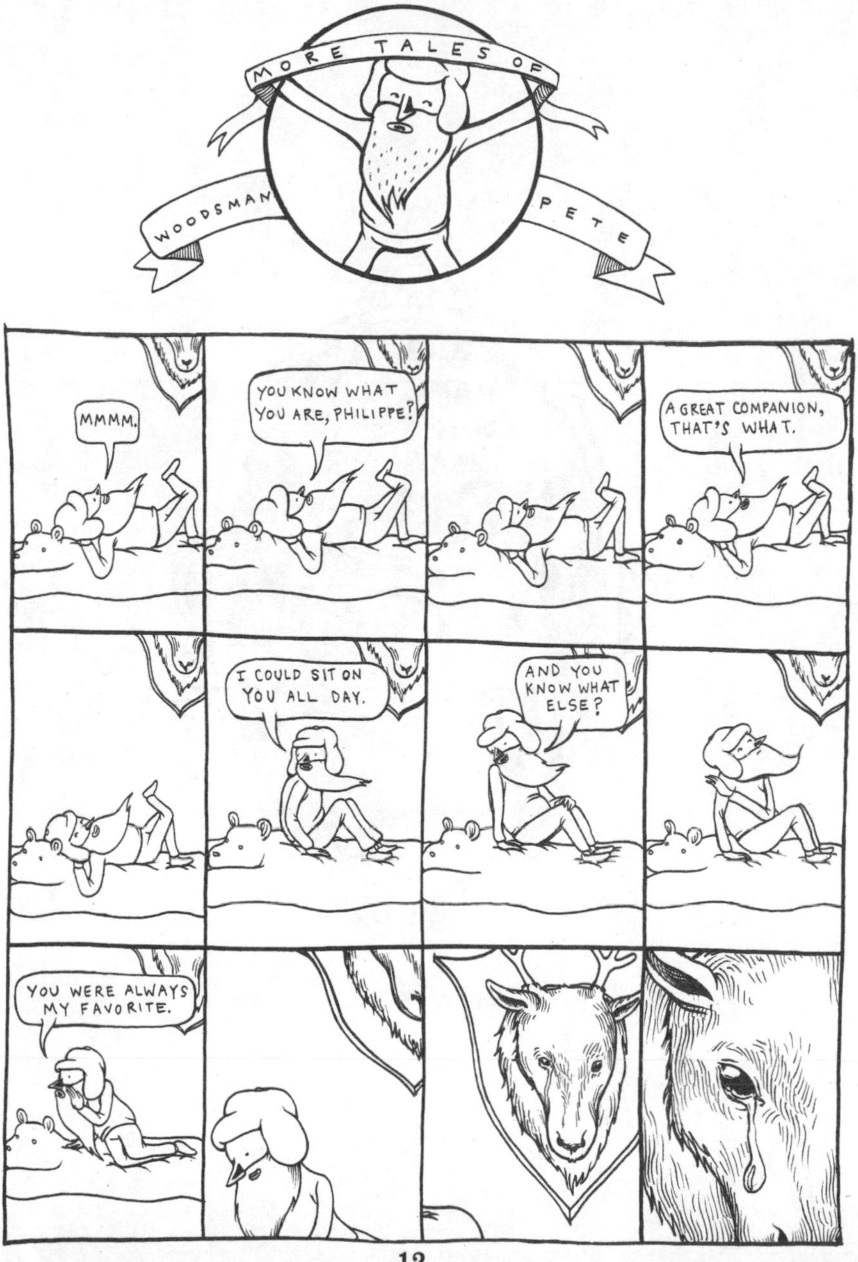
MORE TALES OF
WOODSMAN PETE
MMMM.
YOU KNOW WHAT YOU ARE, PHILIPPE?
A GREAT COMPANION, THAT'S WHAT.
I COULD SIT ON YOU ALL DAY.
AND YOU KNOW WHAT ELSE?
YOU WERE ALWAYS MY FAVORITE.

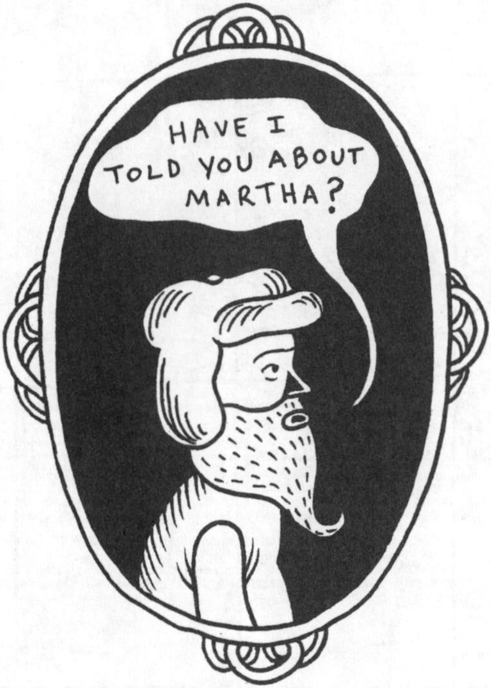
HAVE I TOLD YOU ABOUT MARTHA?

THE DEATH OF PETE'S WIFE, VERSION ONE

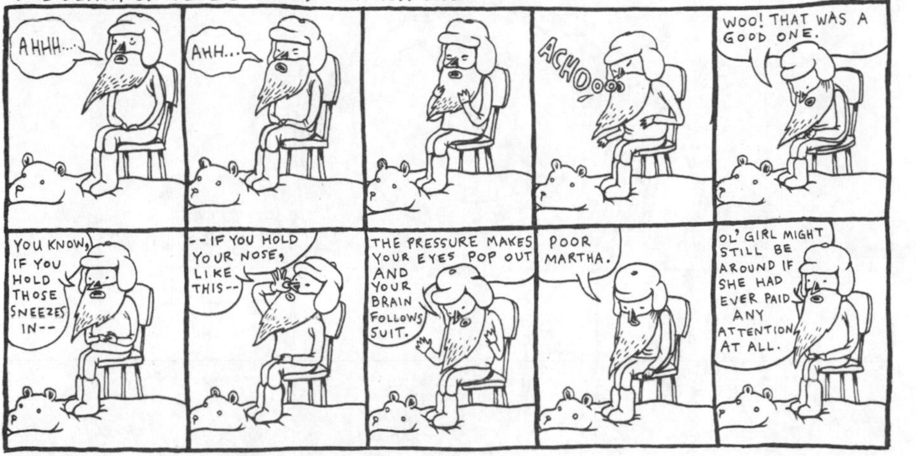
AHHH...
AHH...
ACHOOOO
WOO! THAT WAS A GOOD ONE.
YOU KNOW, IF YOU HOLD THOSE SNEEZES IN--
--IF YOU HOLD YOUR NOSE, LIKE THIS--
THE PRESSURE MAKES YOUR EYES POP OUT AND YOUR BRAIN FOLLOWS SUIT.
POOR MARTHA.
OL' GIRL MIGHT STILL BE AROUND IF SHE HAD EVER PAID ANY ATTENTION AT ALL.

THE DEATH OF PETE'S WIFE, VERSION TWO

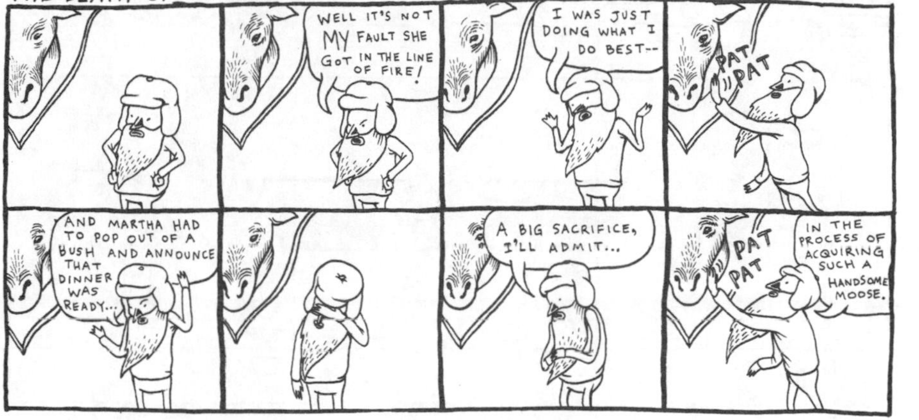
WELL IT'S NOT MY FAULT SHE GOT IN THE LINE OF FIRE!
I WAS JUST DOING WHAT I DO BEST--
PAT PAT
AND MARTHA HAD TO POP OUT OF A BUSH AND ANNOUNCE THAT DINNER WAS READY...
A BIG SACRIFICE, I'LL ADMIT...
PAT PAT
IN THE PROCESS OF ACQUIRING SUCH A HANDSOME MOOSE.

THE DEATH OF PETE'S WIFE, VERSION THREE

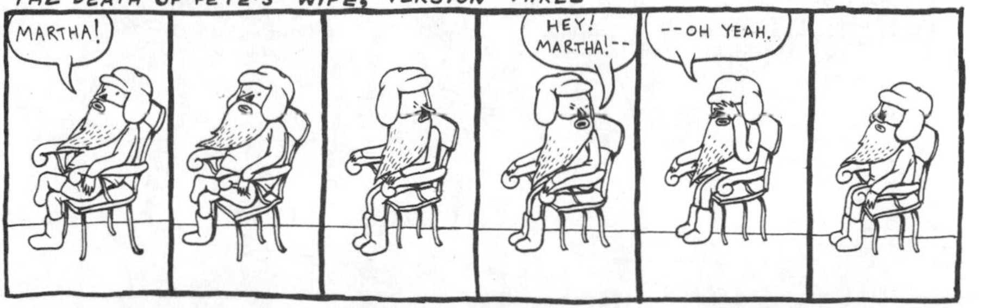
MARTHA!
HEY! MARTHA!--
--OH YEAH.

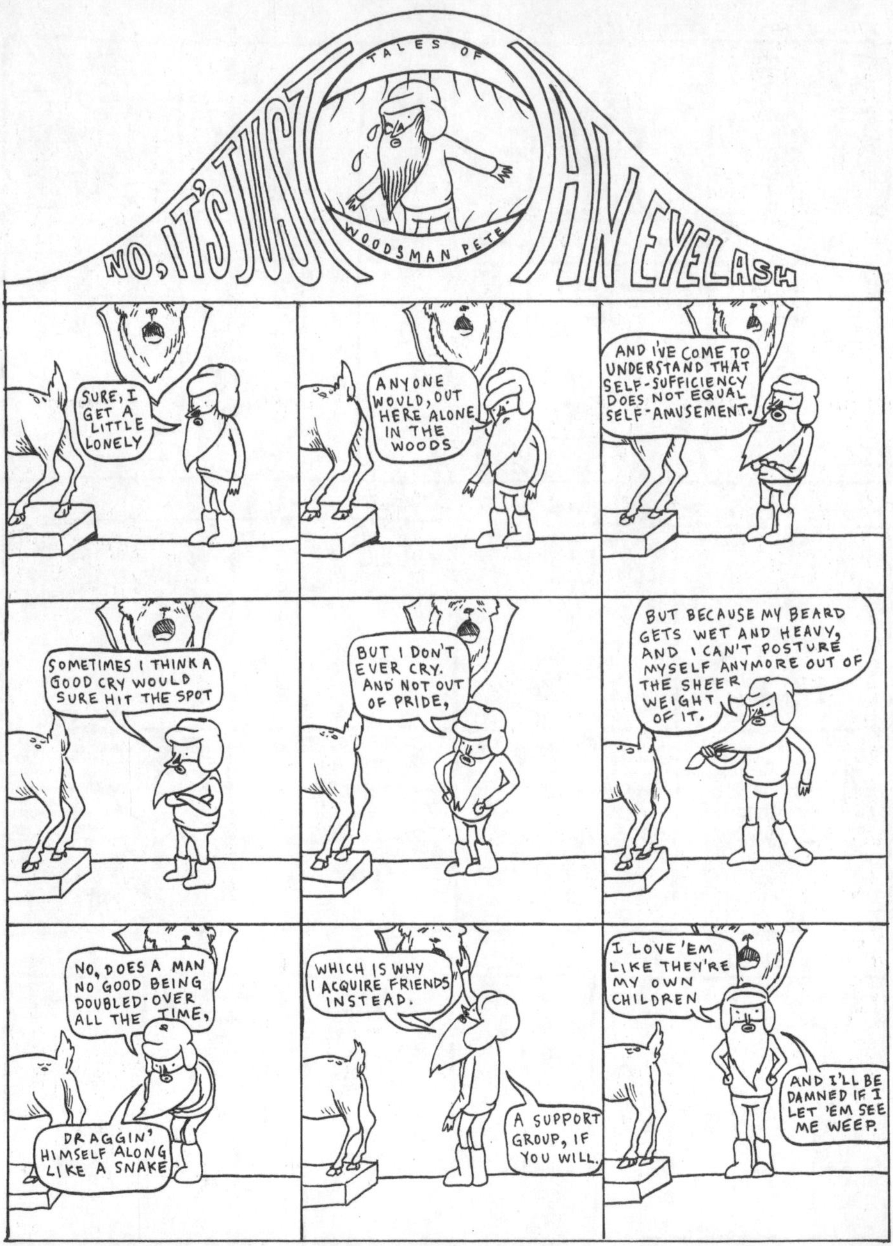
TALES OF WOODSMAN PETE
NO, IT'S JUST AN EYELASH
SURE, I GET A LITTLE LONELY
ANYONE WOULD, OUT HERE ALONE IN THE WOODS
AND I'VE COME TO UNDERSTAND THAT SELF-SUFFICIENCY DOES NOT EQUAL SELF-AMUSEMENT.
SOMETIMES I THINK A GOOD CRY WOULD SURE HIT THE SPOT
BUT I DON'T EVER CRY. AND NOT OUT OF PRIDE,
BUT BECAUSE MY BEARD GETS WET AND HEAVY, AND I CAN'T POSTURE MYSELF ANYMORE OUT OF THE SHEER WEIGHT OF IT.
NO, DOES A MAN NO GOOD BEING DOUBLED-OVER ALL THE TIME,
DRAGGIN' HIMSELF ALONG LIKE A SNAKE
WHICH IS WHY I ACQUIRE FRIENDS INSTEAD.
A SUPPORT GROUP, IF YOU WILL.
I LOVE 'EM LIKE THEY'RE MY OWN CHILDREN
AND I'LL BE DAMNED IF I LET 'EM SEE ME WEEP.

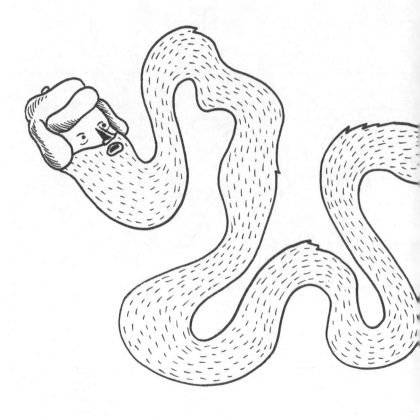

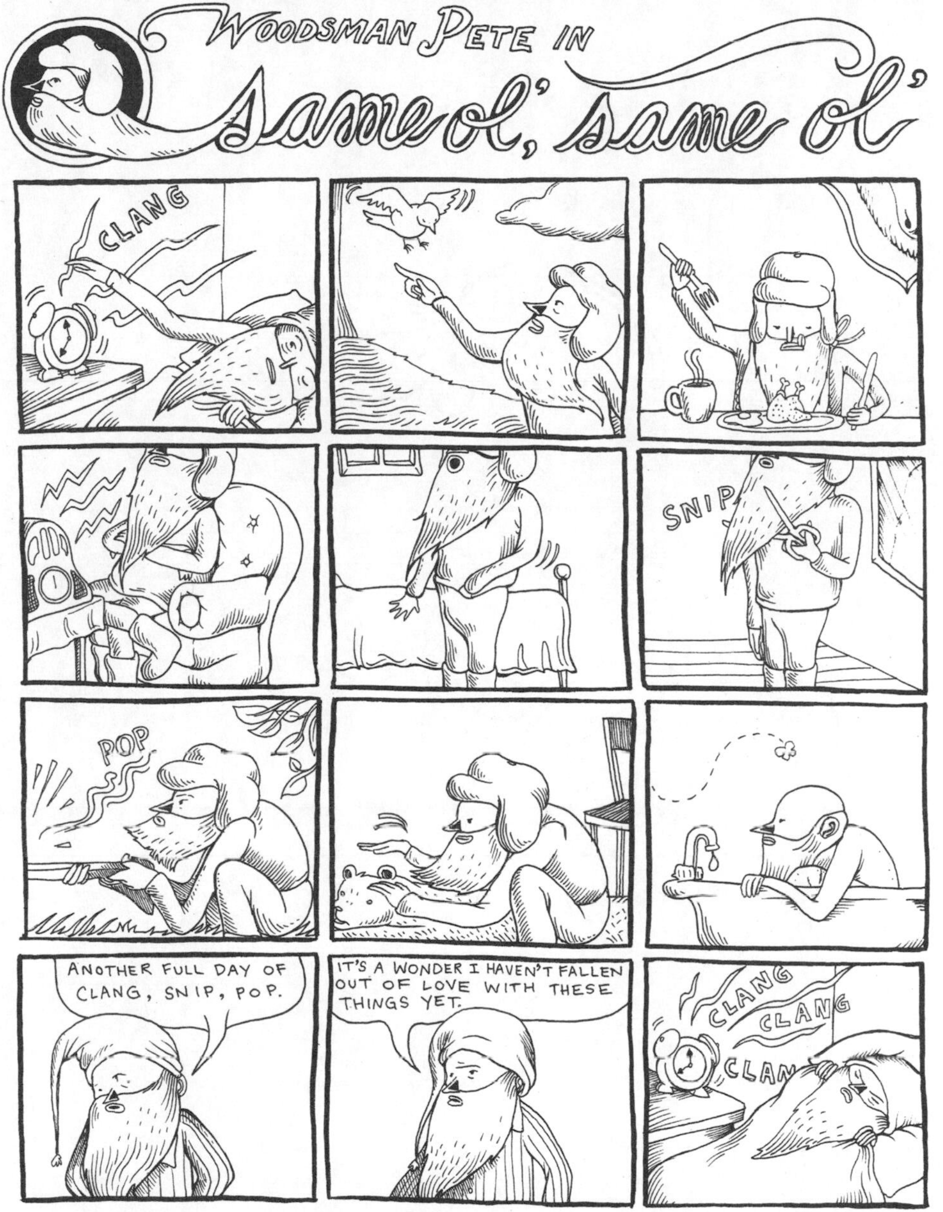
WOODSMAN PETE IN
same ol', same ol'
CLANG
SNIP
POP
ANOTHER FULL DAY OF CLANG, SNIP, POP.
IT'S A WONDER I HAVEN'T FALLEN OUT OF LOVE WITH THESE THINGS YET.
CLANG
CLANG
CLAN

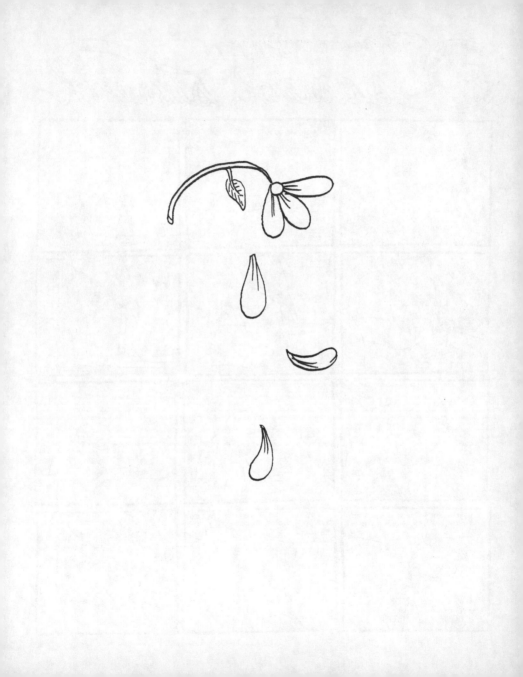

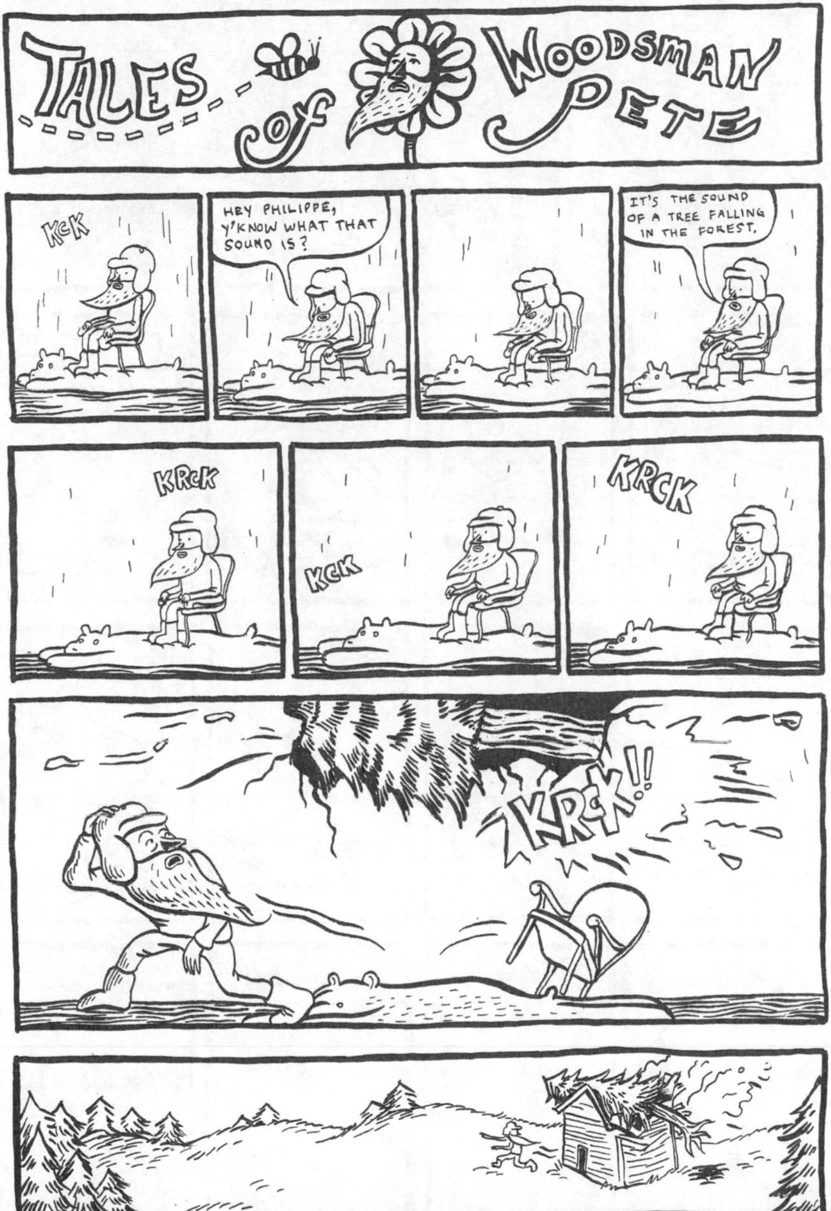
TALES of WOODSMAN PETE
KCK
HEY PHILIPPE, Y'KNOW WHAT THAT SOUND IS?
IT'S THE SOUND OF A TREE FALLING IN THE FOREST.
KRCK
KCK
KRCK
KRCK!!

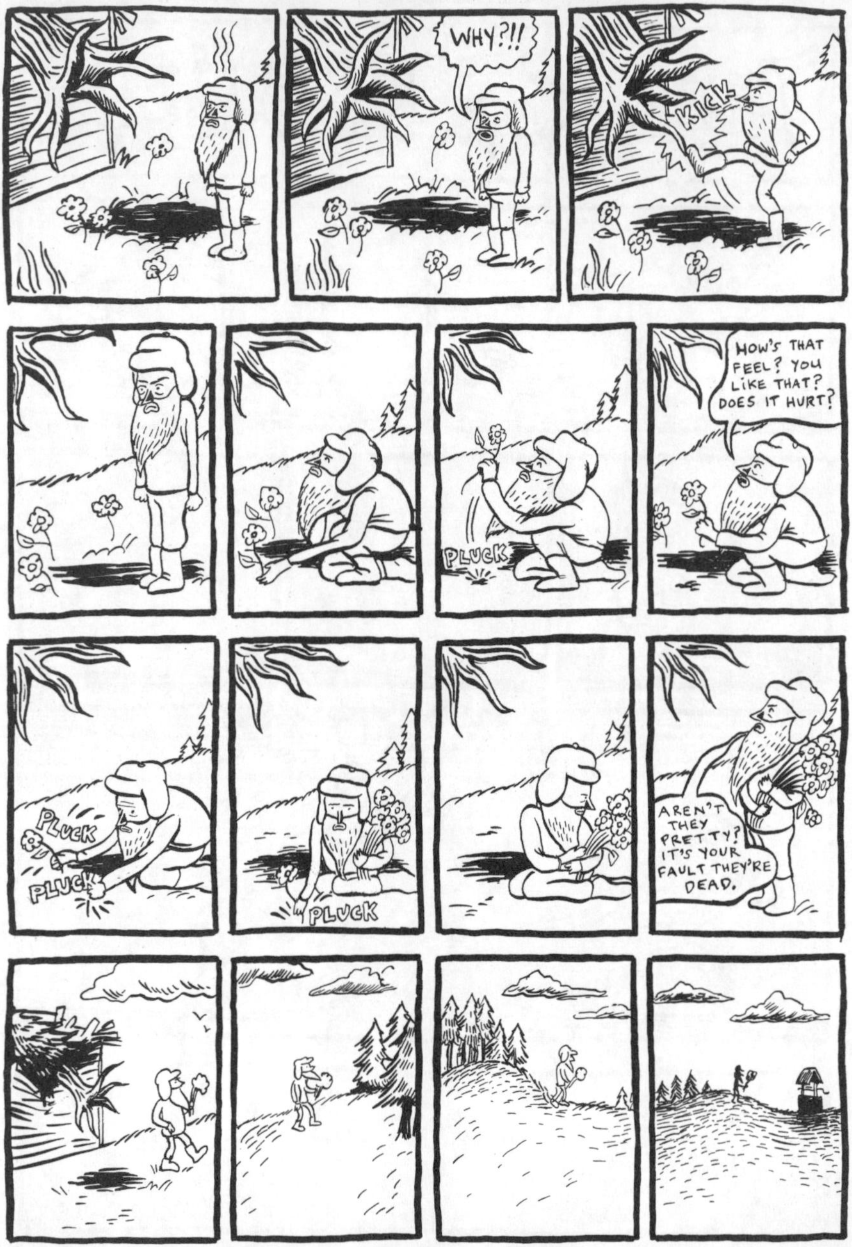
WHY?!!
KICK
PLUCK
HOW'S THAT FEEL? YOU LIKE THAT? DOES IT HURT?
PLUCK
PLUCK
PLUCK
AREN'T THEY PRETTY? IT'S YOUR FAULT THEY'RE DEAD.

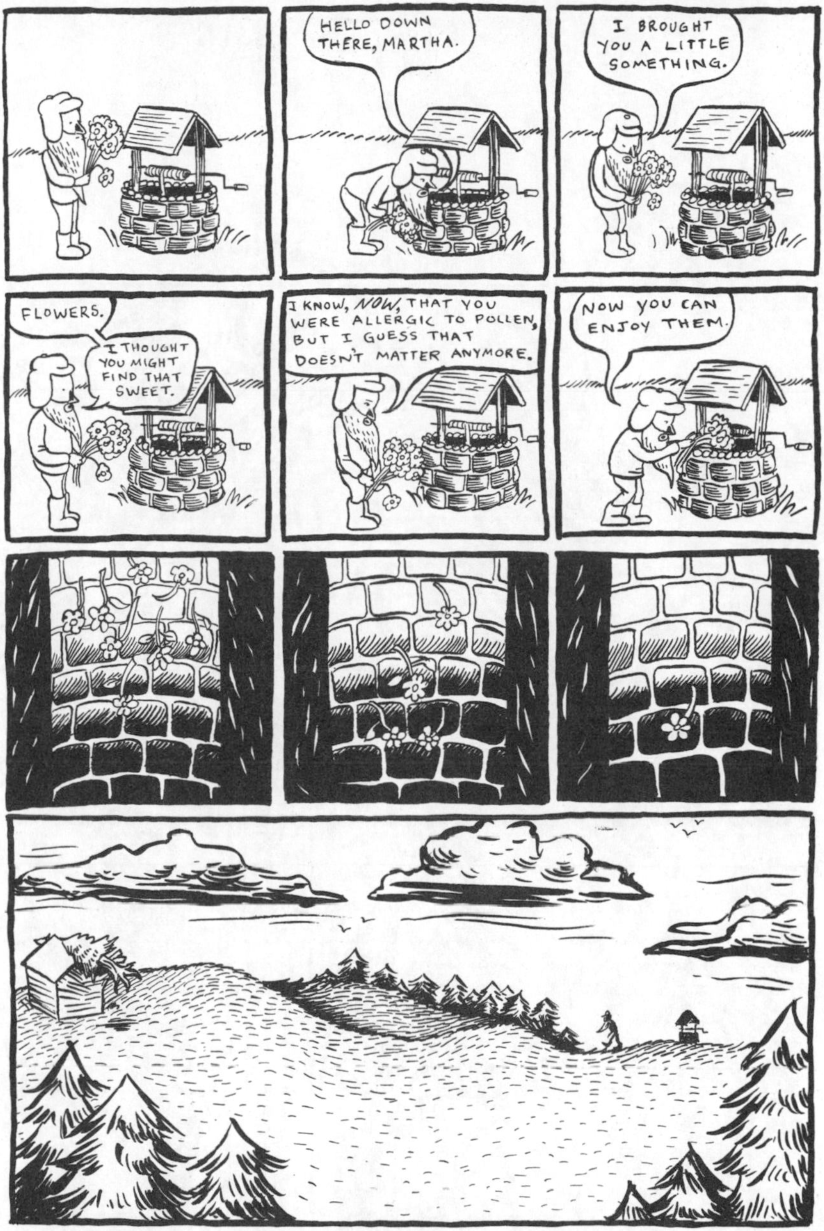
HELLO DOWN THERE, MARTHA.
I BROUGHT YOU A LITTLE SOMETHING.
FLOWERS.
I THOUGHT YOU MIGHT FIND THAT SWEET.
I KNOW, NOW, THAT YOU WERE ALLERGIC TO POLLEN, BUT I GUESS THAT DOESN'T MATTER ANYMORE.
NOW YOU CAN ENJOY THEM.

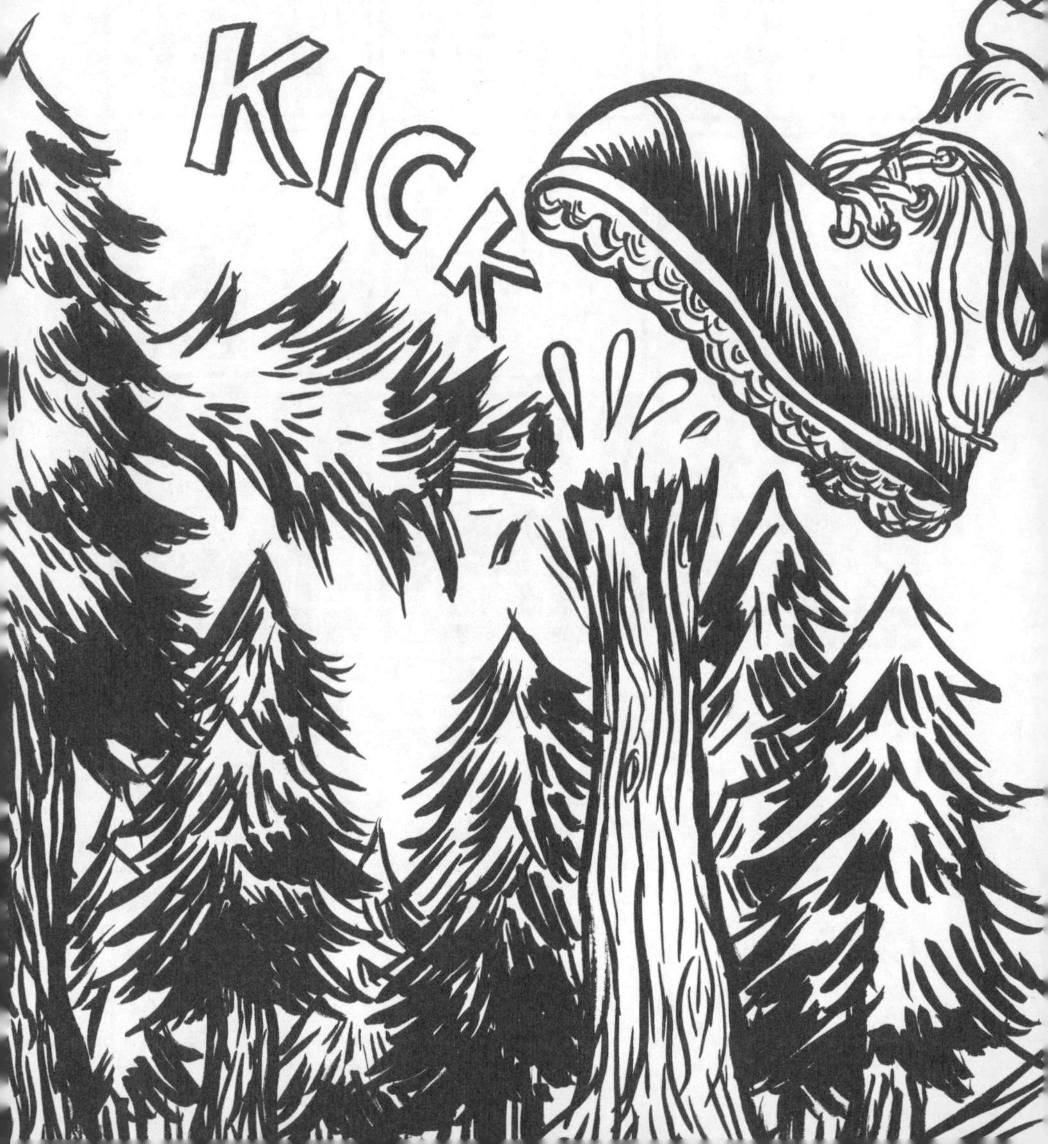
KICK

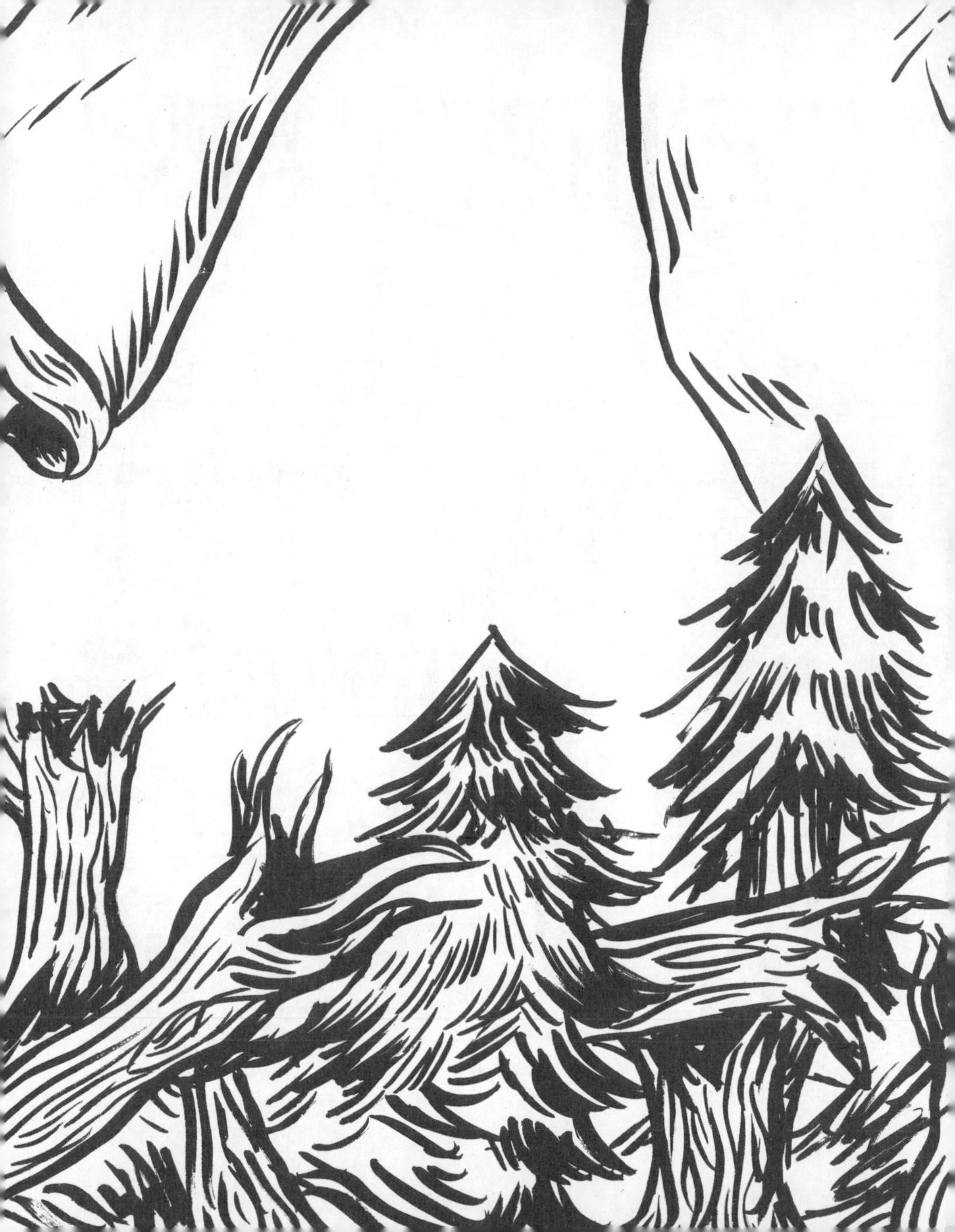

ADVENTURES of PAUL BUNYAN & HIS OX, BABE

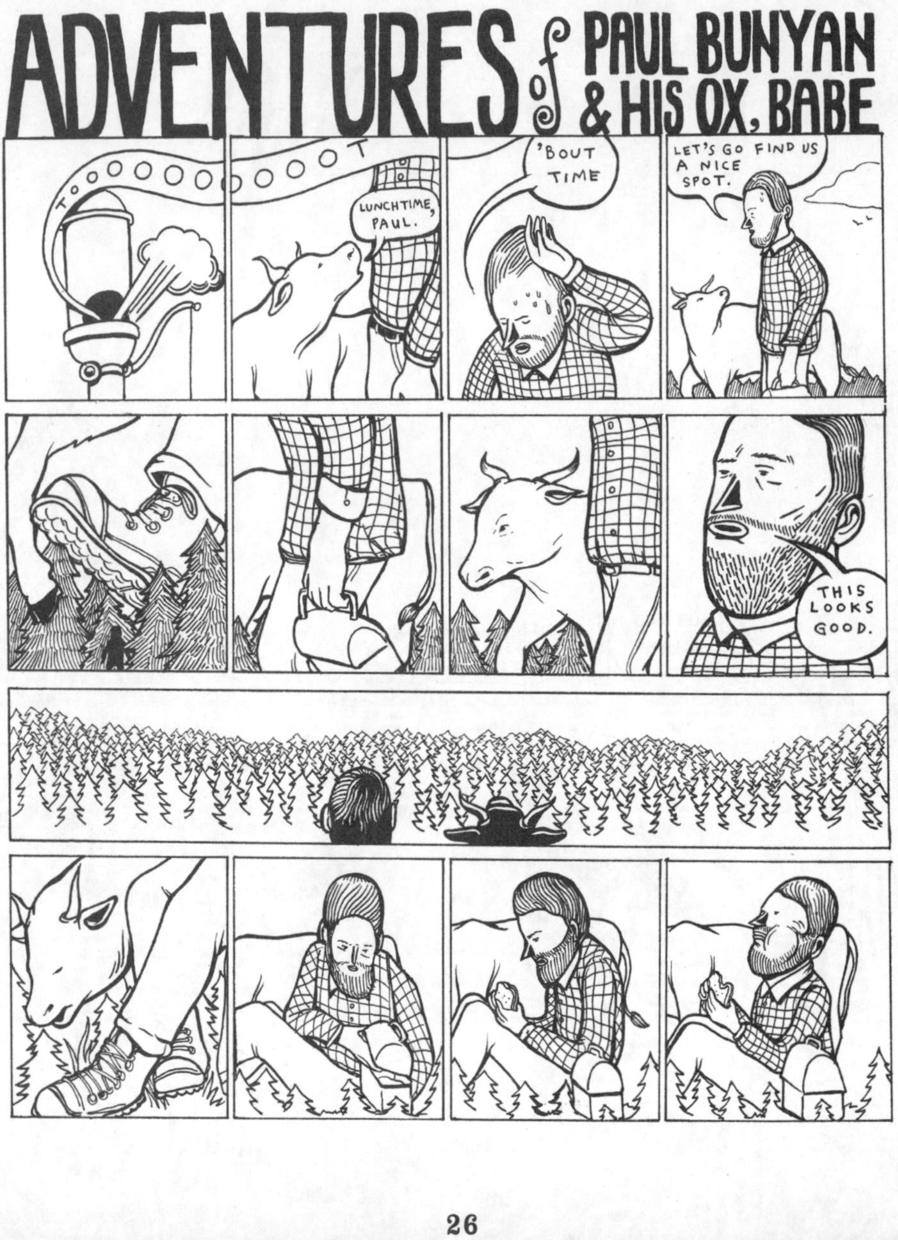
TOOOOOOOOOOOT
LUNCHTIME, PAUL.
'BOUT TIME
LET'S GO FIND US A NICE SPOT.
THIS LOOKS GOOD.

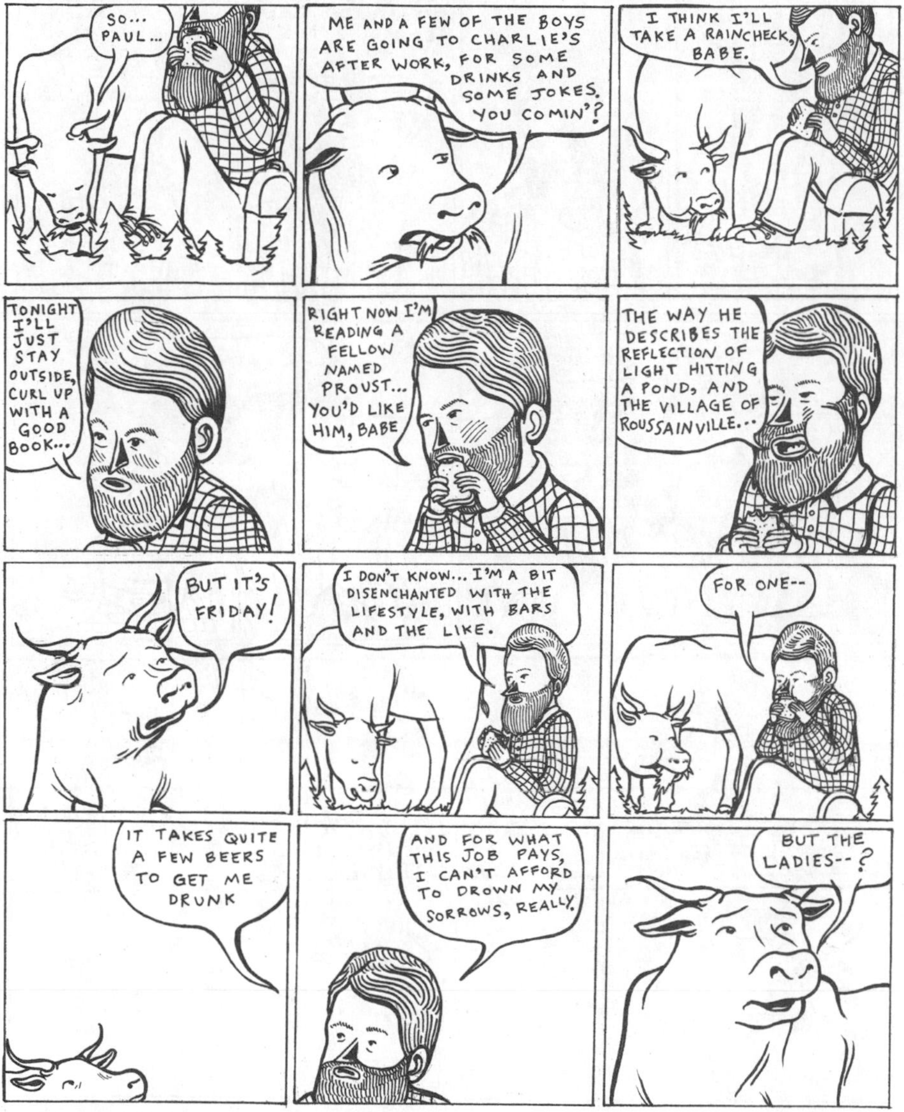
SO... PAUL...
ME AND A FEW OF THE BOYS ARE GOING TO CHARLIE'S AFTER WORK, FOR SOME DRINKS AND SOME JOKES. YOU COMIN'?
I THINK I'LL TAKE A RAINCHECK, BABE.
TONIGHT I'LL JUST STAY OUTSIDE, CURL UP WITH A GOOD BOOK...
RIGHT NOW I'M READING A FELLOW NAMED PROUST... YOU'D LIKE HIM, BABE
THE WAY HE DESCRIBES THE REFLECTION OF LIGHT HITTING A POND, AND THE VILLAGE OF ROUSSAINVILLE...
BUT IT'S FRIDAY!
I DON'T KNOW... I'M A BIT DISENCHANTED WITH THE LIFESTYLE, WITH BARS AND THE LIKE.
FOR ONE--
IT TAKES QUITE A FEW BEERS TO GET ME DRUNK
AND FOR WHAT THIS JOB PAYS, I CAN'T AFFORD TO DROWN MY SORROWS, REALLY.
BUT THE LADIES--?

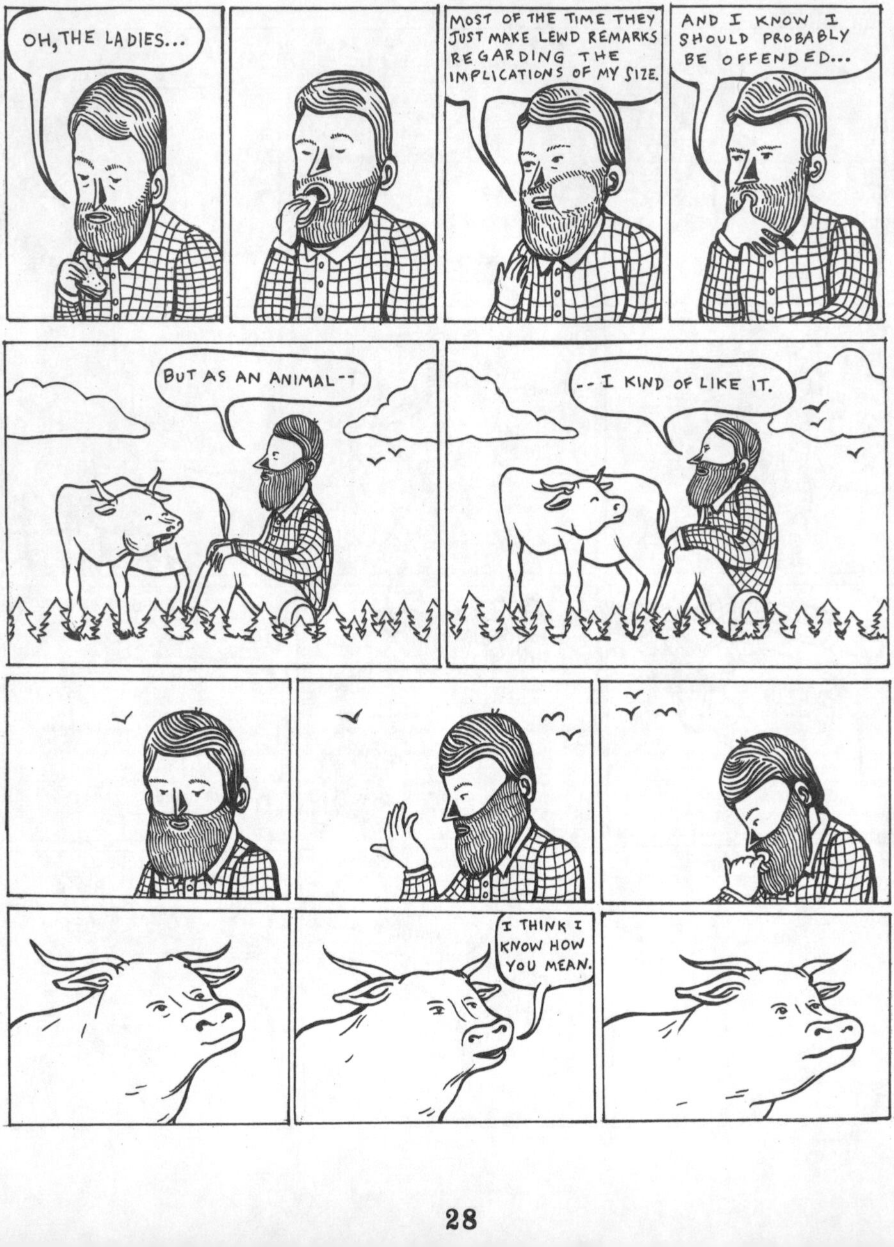
OH, THE LADIES...
MOST OF THE TIME THEY JUST MAKE LEWD REMARKS REGARDING THE IMPLICATIONS OF MY SIZE.
AND I KNOW I SHOULD PROBABLY BE OFFENDED...
BUT AS AN ANIMAL--
--I KIND OF LIKE IT.
I THINK I KNOW HOW YOU MEAN.

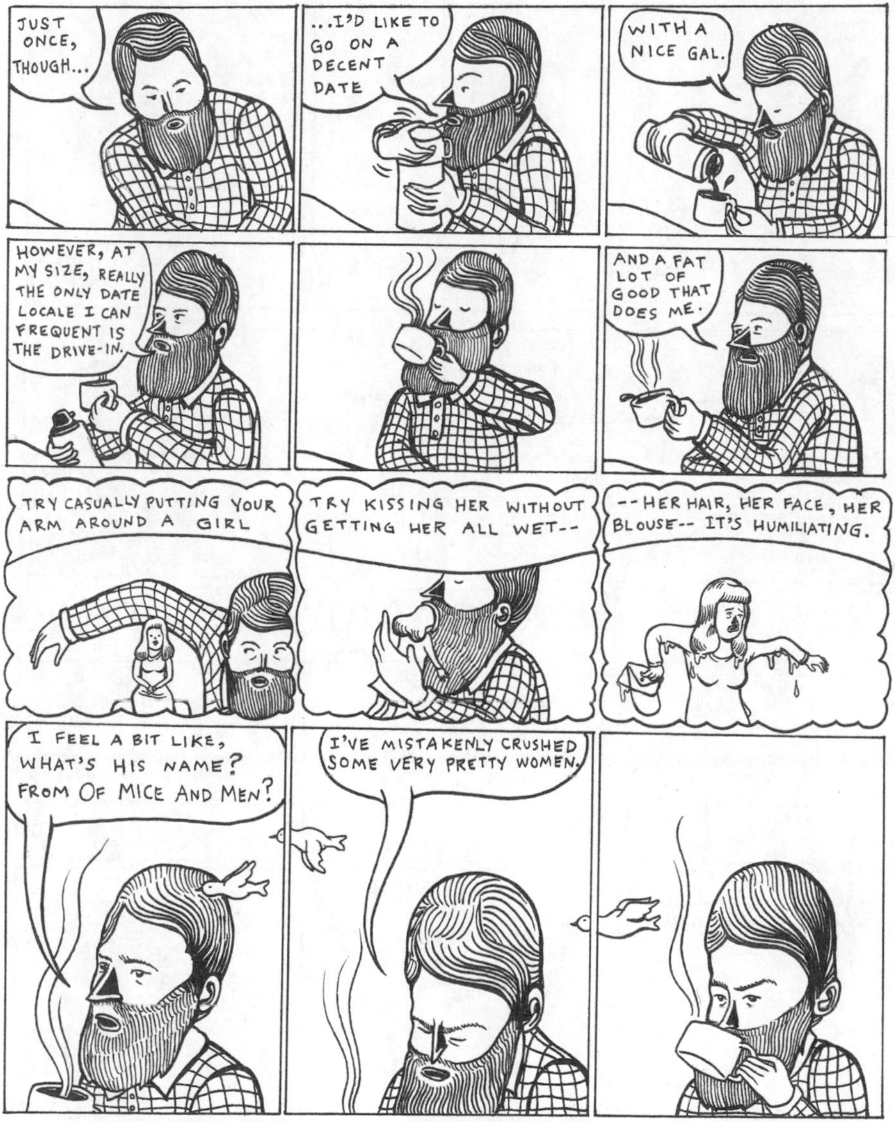
JUST ONCE, THOUGH...
...I'D LIKE TO GO ON A DECENT DATE
WITH A NICE GAL.
HOWEVER, AT MY SIZE, REALLY THE ONLY DATE LOCALE I CAN FREQUENT IS THE DRIVE-IN.
AND A FAT LOT OF GOOD THAT DOES ME.
TRY CASUALLY PUTTING YOUR ARM AROUND A GIRL
TRY KISSING HER WITHOUT GETTING HER ALL WET--
--HER HAIR, HER FACE, HER BLOUSE-- IT'S HUMILIATING.
I FEEL A BIT LIKE, WHAT'S HIS NAME? FROM OF MICE AND MEN?
I'VE MISTAKENLY CRUSHED SOME VERY PRETTY WOMEN.

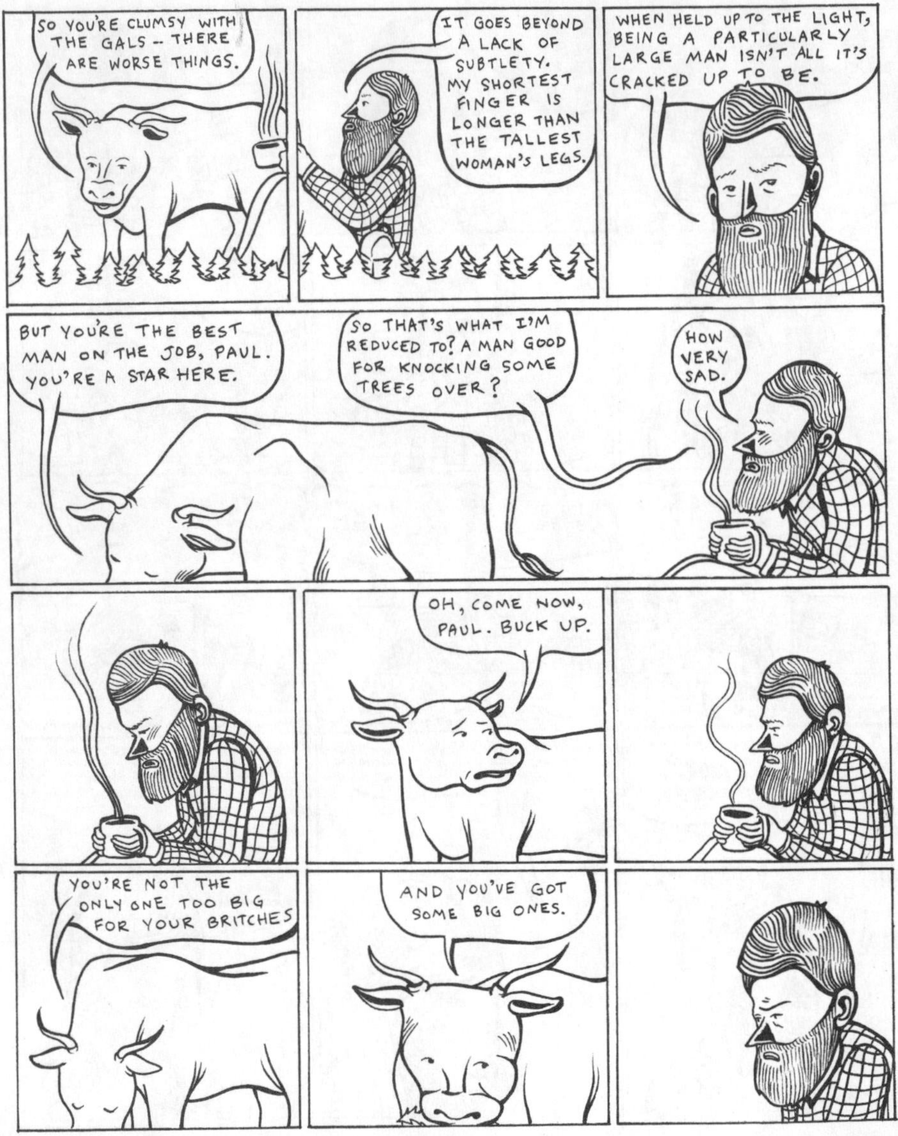
SO YOU'RE CLUMSY WITH THE GALS -- THERE ARE WORSE THINGS.
IT GOES BEYOND A LACK OF SUBTLETY. MY SHORTEST FINGER IS LONGER THAN THE TALLEST WOMAN'S LEGS.
WHEN HELD UP TO THE LIGHT, BEING A PARTICULARLY LARGE MAN ISN'T ALL IT'S CRACKED UP TO BE.
BUT YOU'RE THE BEST MAN ON THE JOB, PAUL. YOU'RE A STAR HERE.
SO THAT'S WHAT I'M REDUCED TO? A MAN GOOD FOR KNOCKING SOME TREES OVER?
HOW VERY SAD.
OH, COME NOW, PAUL. BUCK UP.
YOU'RE NOT THE ONLY ONE TOO BIG FOR YOUR BRITCHES
AND YOU'VE GOT SOME BIG ONES.

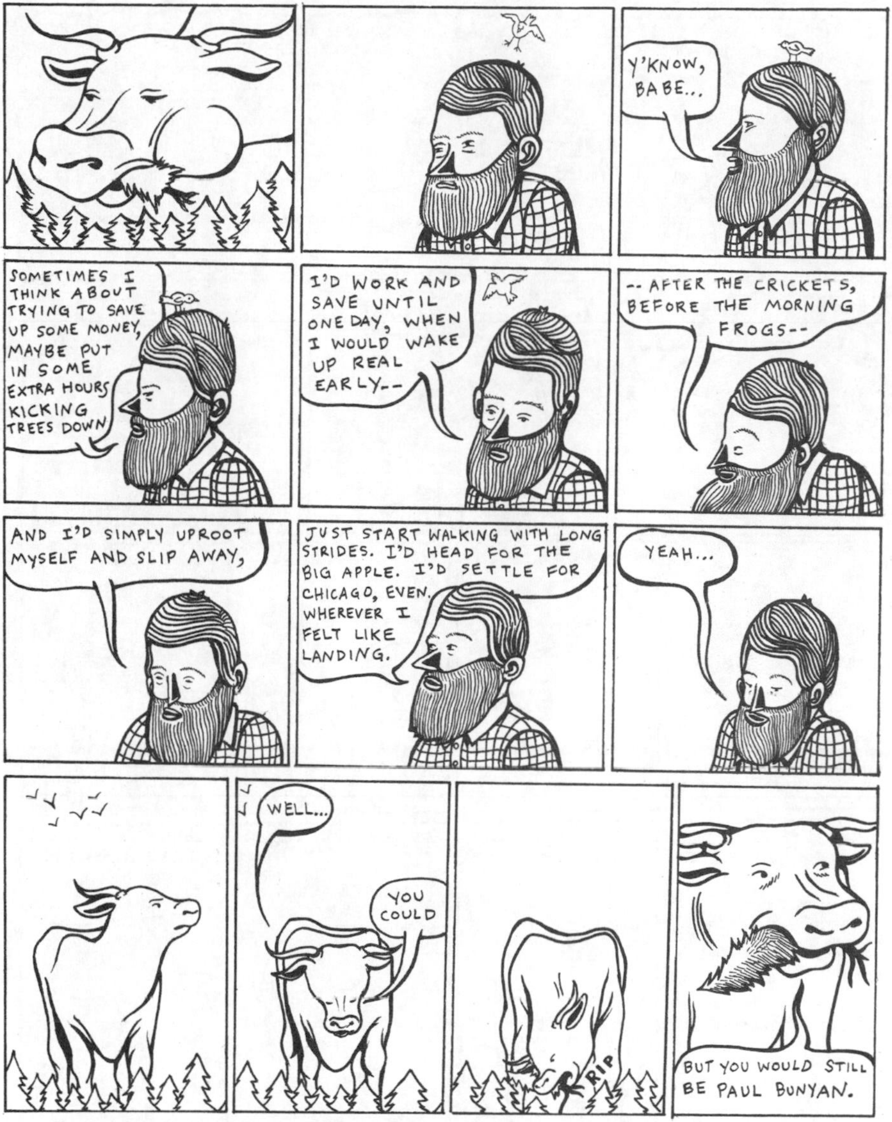
Y'KNOW, BABE...
SOMETIMES I THINK ABOUT TRYING TO SAVE UP SOME MONEY, MAYBE PUT IN SOME EXTRA HOURS KICKING TREES DOWN
I'D WORK AND SAVE UNTIL ONE DAY, WHEN I WOULD WAKE UP REAL EARLY--
-- AFTER THE CRICKETS, BEFORE THE MORNING FROGS--
AND I'D SIMPLY UPROOT MYSELF AND SLIP AWAY,
JUST START WALKING WITH LONG STRIDES. I'D HEAD FOR THE BIG APPLE. I'D SETTLE FOR CHICAGO, EVEN. WHEREVER I FELT LIKE LANDING.
YEAH...
WELL...
YOU COULD
RIP
BUT YOU WOULD STILL BE PAUL BUNYAN.

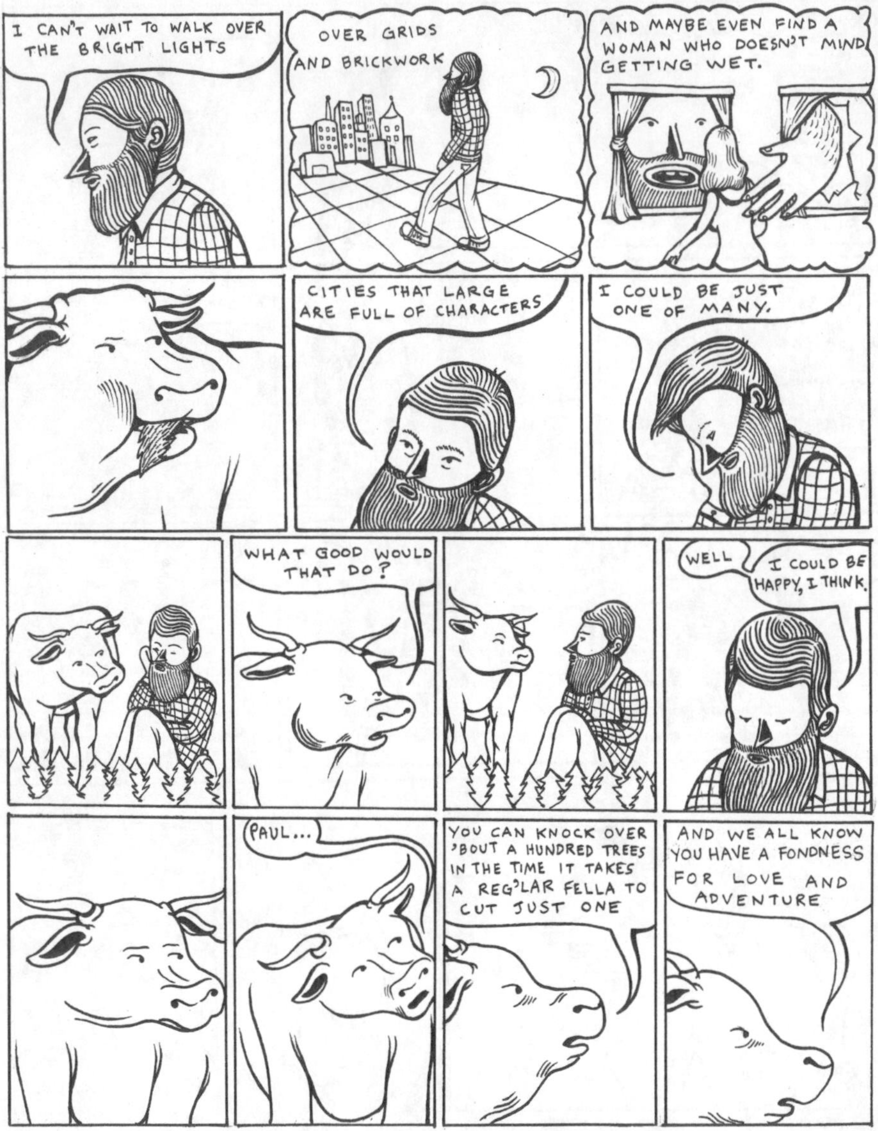
I CAN'T WAIT TO WALK OVER THE BRIGHT LIGHTS
OVER GRIDS
AND BRICKWORK
AND MAYBE EVEN FIND A WOMAN WHO DOESN'T MIND GETTING WET.
CITIES THAT LARGE ARE FULL OF CHARACTERS
I COULD BE JUST ONE OF MANY.
WHAT GOOD WOULD THAT DO?
WELL
I COULD BE HAPPY, I THINK.
PAUL...
YOU CAN KNOCK OVER 'BOUT A HUNDRED TREES IN THE TIME IT TAKES A REG'LAR FELLA TO CUT JUST ONE
AND WE ALL KNOW YOU HAVE A FONDNESS FOR LOVE AND ADVENTURE

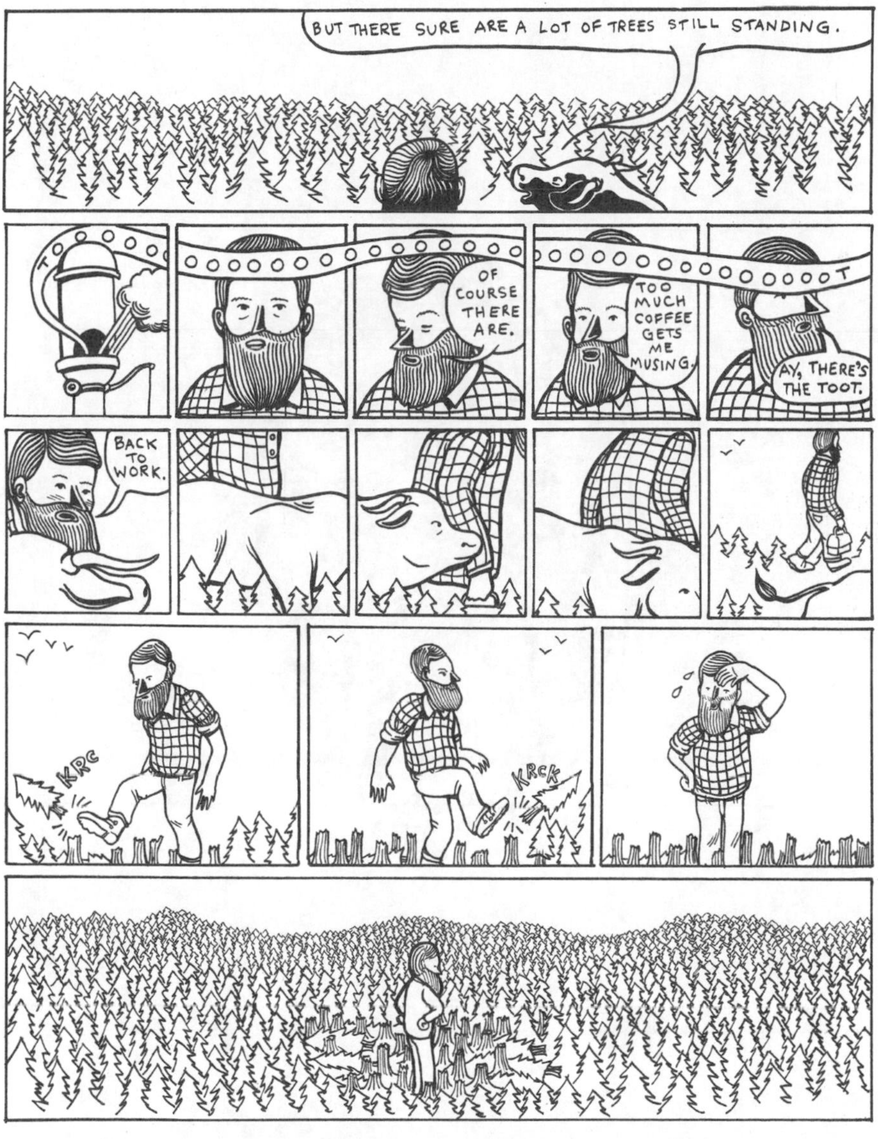
BUT THERE SURE ARE A LOT OF TREES STILL STANDING.
TOOOOOOOOOOOOOOOOOOOOOOOOOOOOOOOOOT
OF COURSE THERE ARE.
TOO MUCH COFFEE GETS ME MUSING.
AY, THERE'S THE TOOT.
BACK TO WORK.
KRC
KRCK

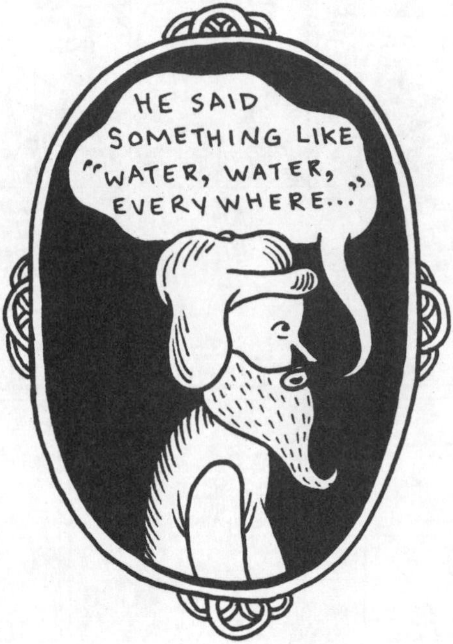
HE SAID SOMETHING LIKE "WATER, WATER, EVERYWHERE..."

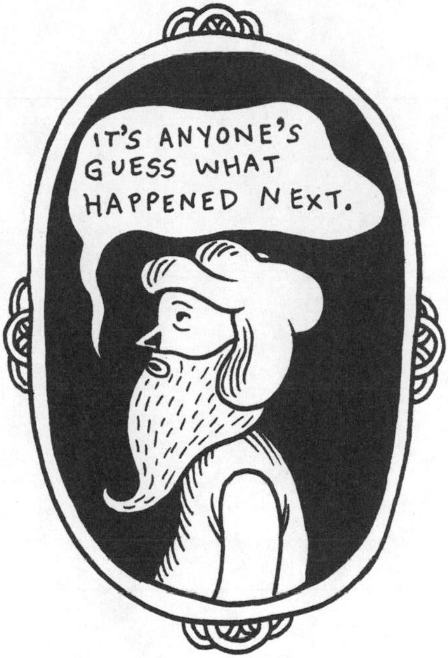
IT'S ANYONE'S GUESS WHAT HAPPENED NEXT.

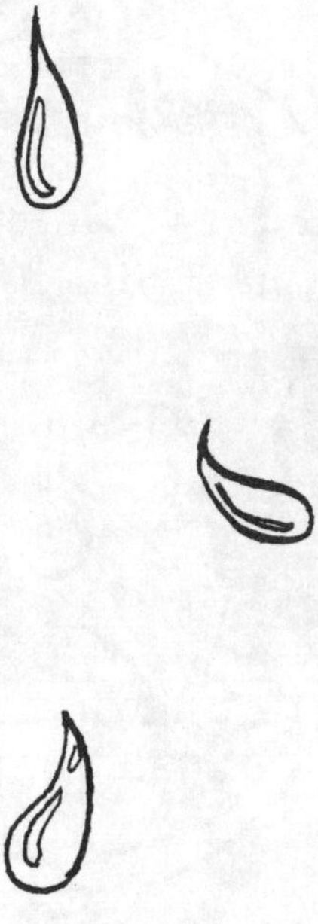

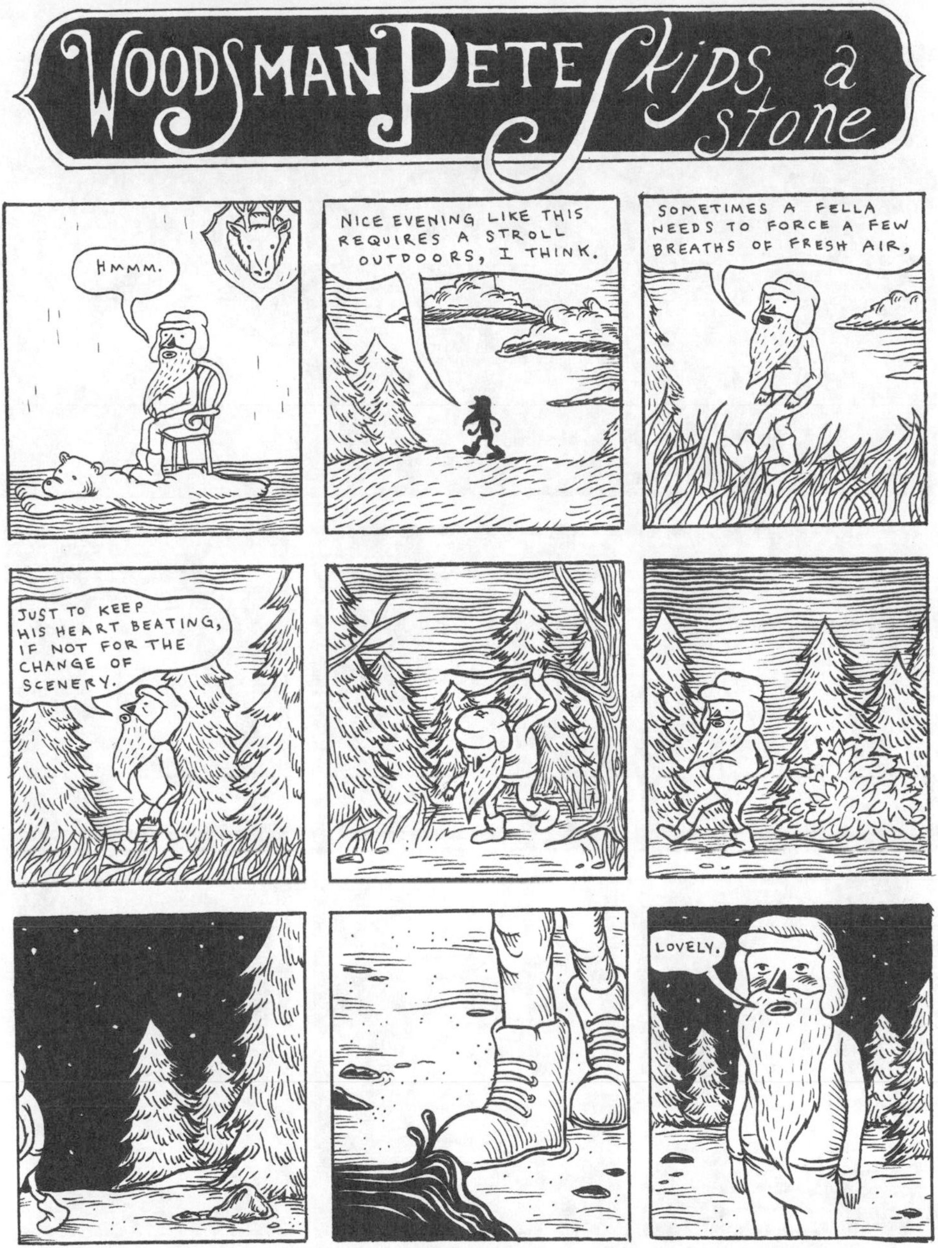
Woodsman Pete Skips a stone
HMMM.
NICE EVENING LIKE THIS REQUIRES A STROLL OUTDOORS, I THINK.
SOMETIMES A FELLA NEEDS TO FORCE A FEW BREATHS OF FRESH AIR,
JUST TO KEEP HIS HEART BEATING, IF NOT FOR THE CHANGE OF SCENERY.
LOVELY.

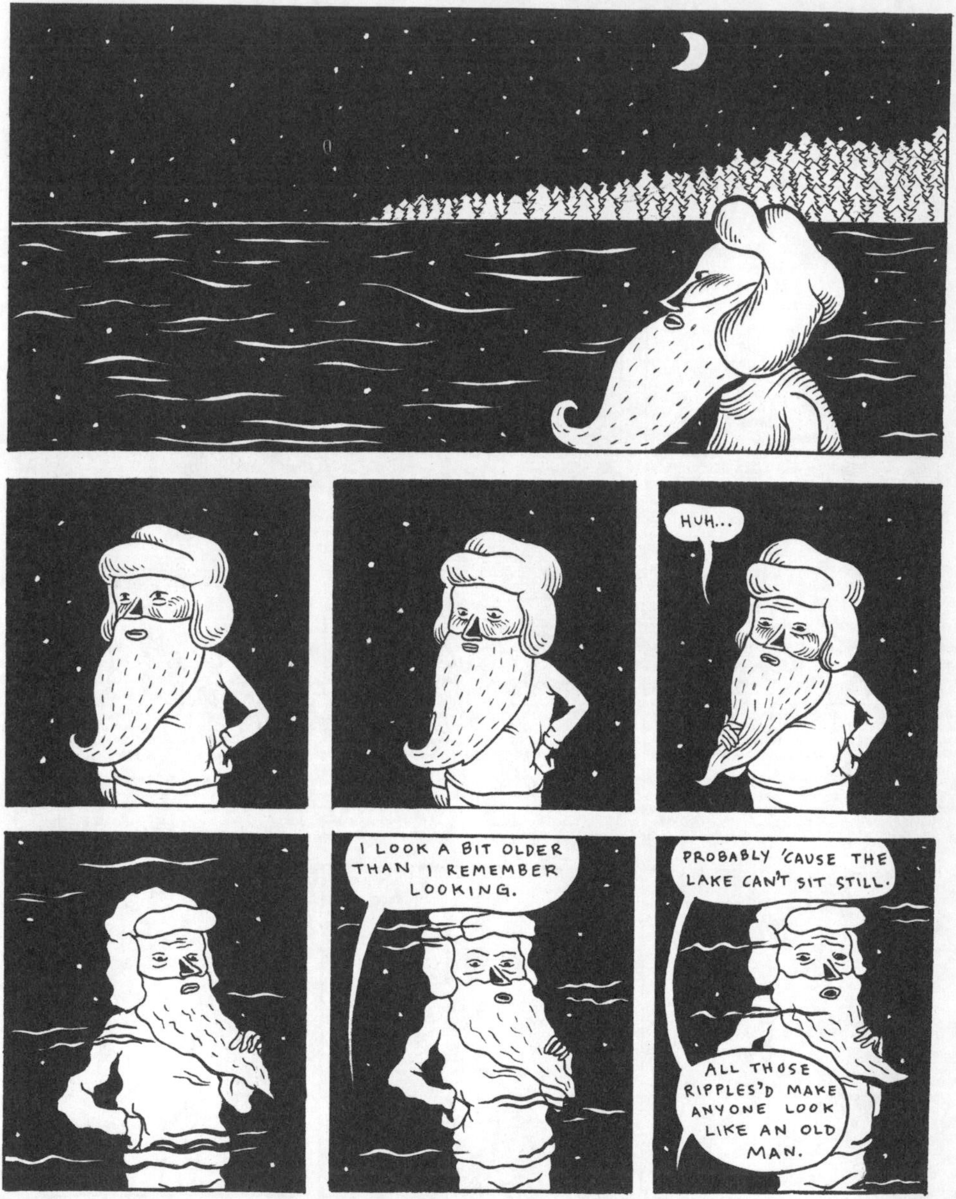
HUH...
I LOOK A BIT OLDER THAN I REMEMBER LOOKING.
PROBABLY 'CAUSE THE LAKE CAN'T SIT STILL.
ALL THOSE RIPPLES'D MAKE ANYONE LOOK LIKE AN OLD MAN.

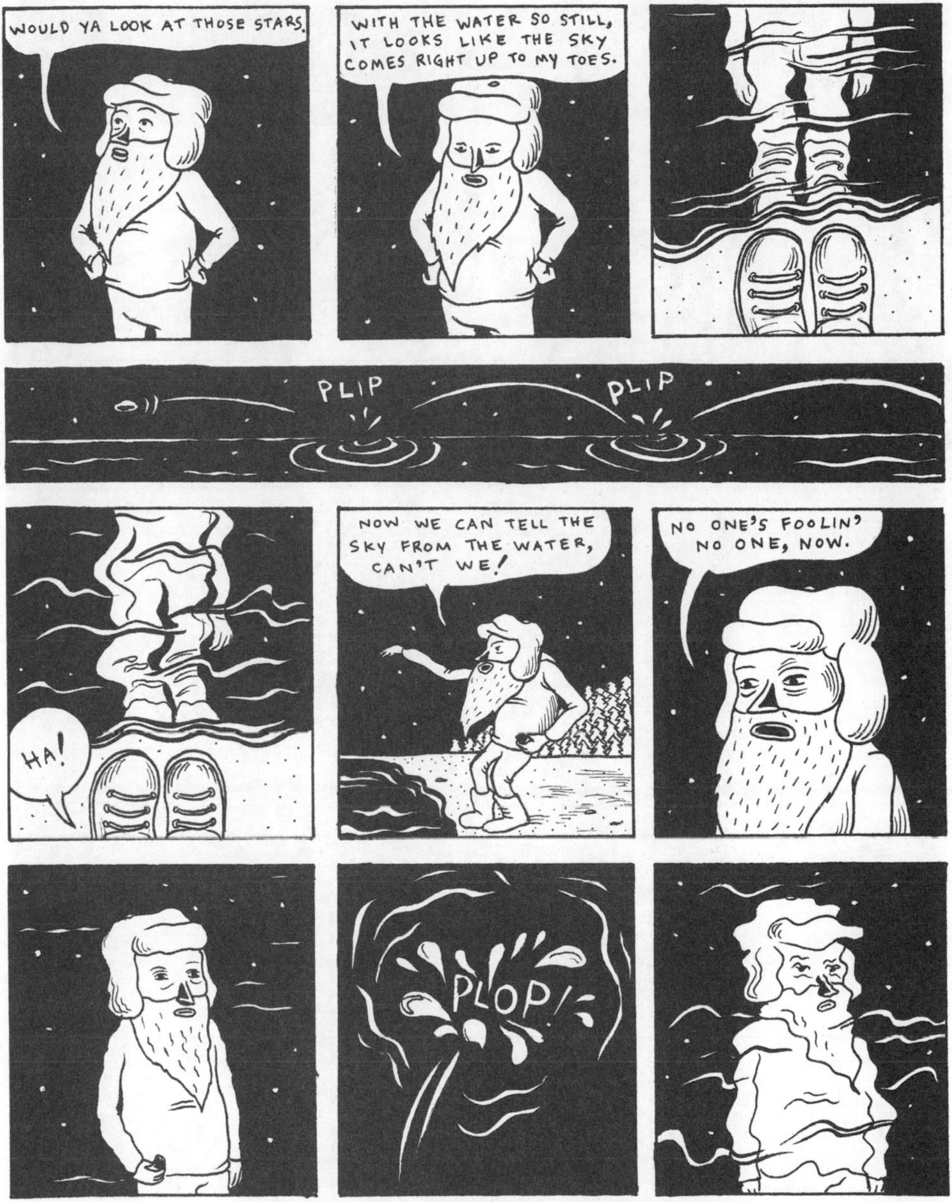
WOULD YA LOOK AT THOSE STARS.
WITH THE WATER SO STILL, IT LOOKS LIKE THE SKY COMES RIGHT UP TO MY TOES.
PLIP
PLIP
HA!
NOW WE CAN TELL THE SKY FROM THE WATER, CAN'T WE!
NO ONE'S FOOLIN' NO ONE, NOW.
PLOP!

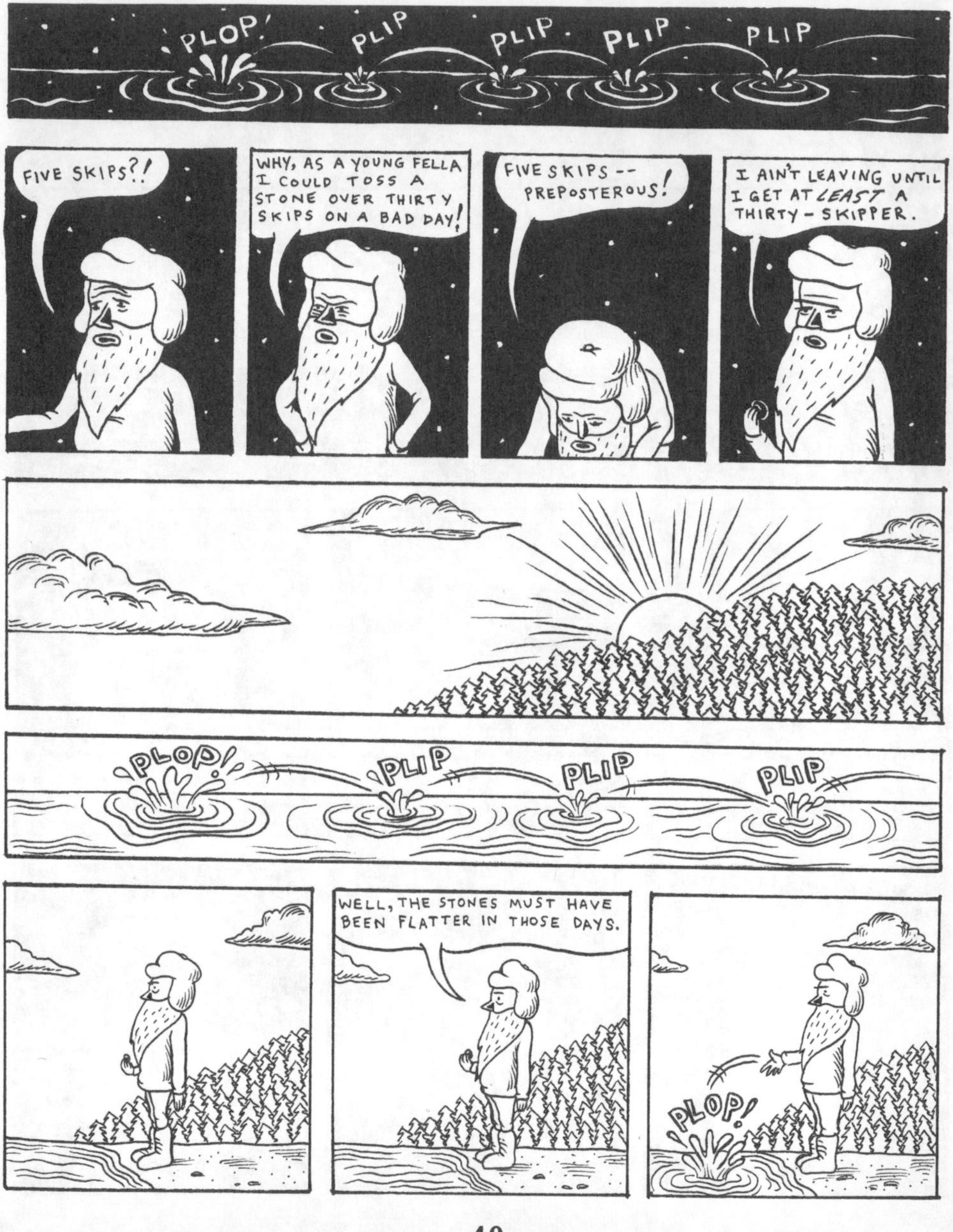
PLOP!
PLIP
PLIP
PLIP
PLIP
FIVE SKIPS?!
WHY, AS A YOUNG FELLA I COULD TOSS A STONE OVER THIRTY SKIPS ON A BAD DAY!
FIVE SKIPS -- PREPOSTEROUS!
I AIN'T LEAVING UNTIL I GET AT LEAST A THIRTY-SKIPPER.
PLOP!
PLIP
PLIP
PLIP
WELL, THE STONES MUST HAVE BEEN FLATTER IN THOSE DAYS.
PLOP!

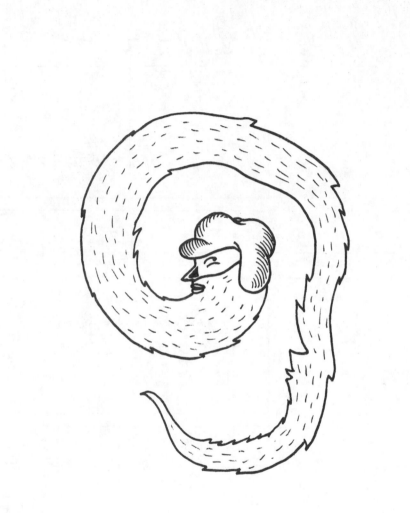

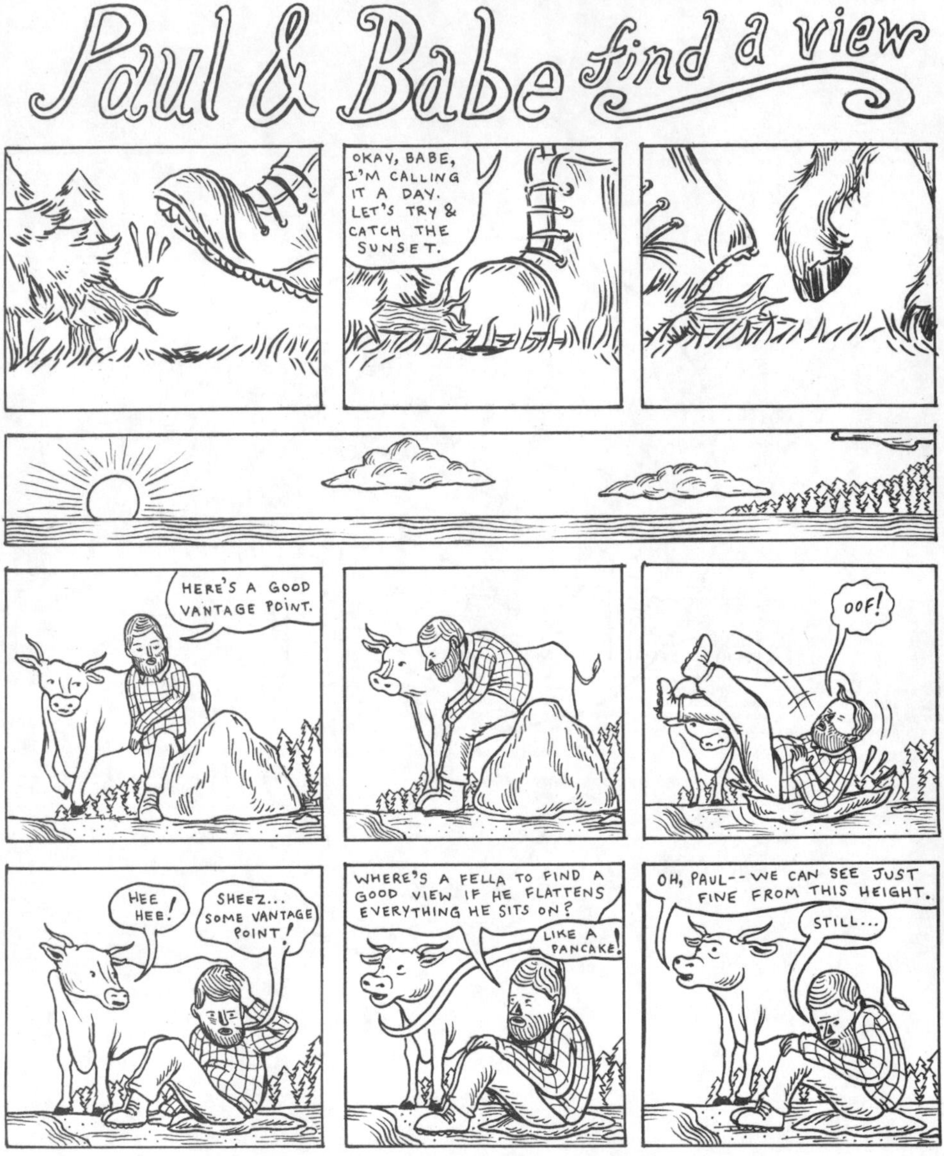
Paul & Babe find a view
OKAY, BABE, I'M CALLING IT A DAY. LET'S TRY & CATCH THE SUNSET.
HERE'S A GOOD VANTAGE POINT.
OOF!
HEE HEE!
SHEEZ... SOME VANTAGE POINT!
WHERE'S A FELLA TO FIND A GOOD VIEW IF HE FLATTENS EVERYTHING HE SITS ON?
LIKE A PANCAKE!
OH, PAUL-- WE CAN SEE JUST FINE FROM THIS HEIGHT.
STILL...

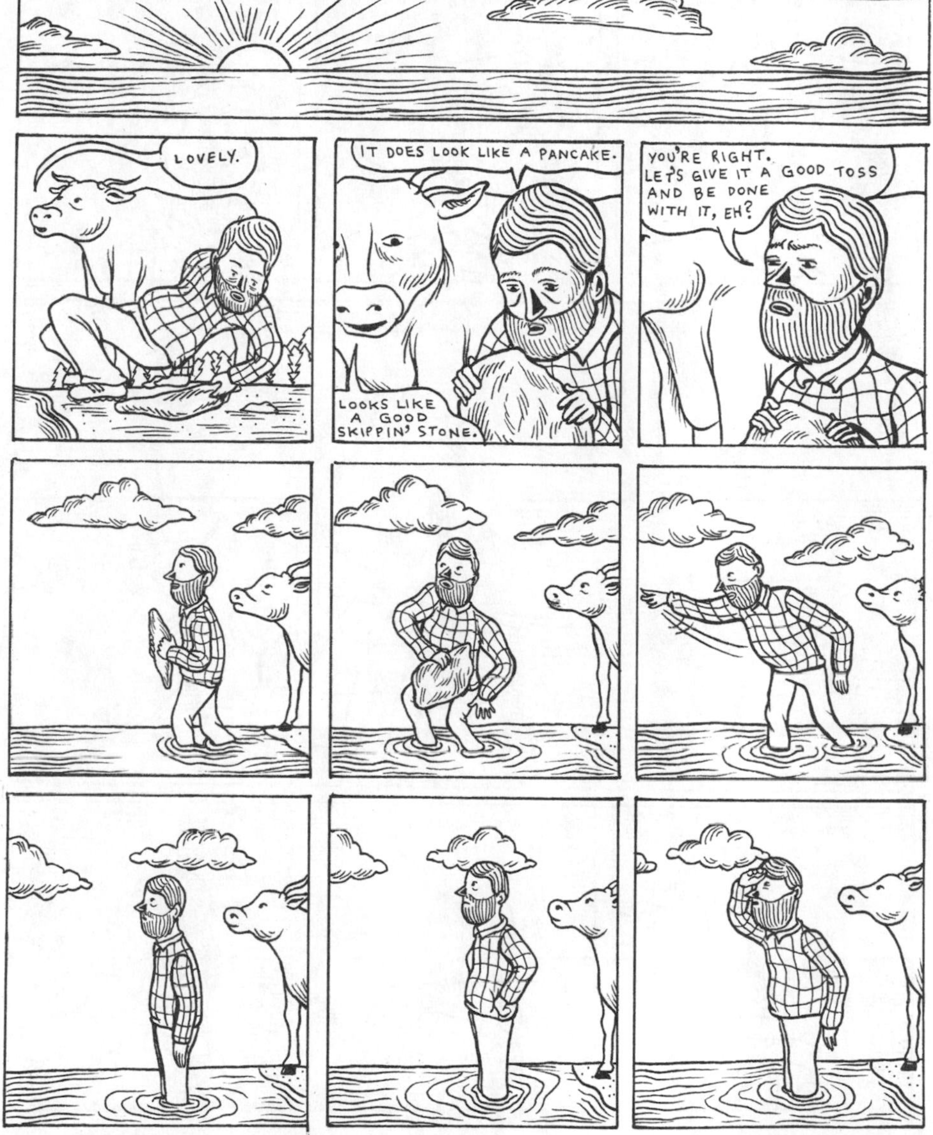
LOVELY.
IT DOES LOOK LIKE A PANCAKE.
LOOKS LIKE A GOOD SKIPPIN' STONE.
YOU'RE RIGHT. LET'S GIVE IT A GOOD TOSS AND BE DONE WITH IT, EH?

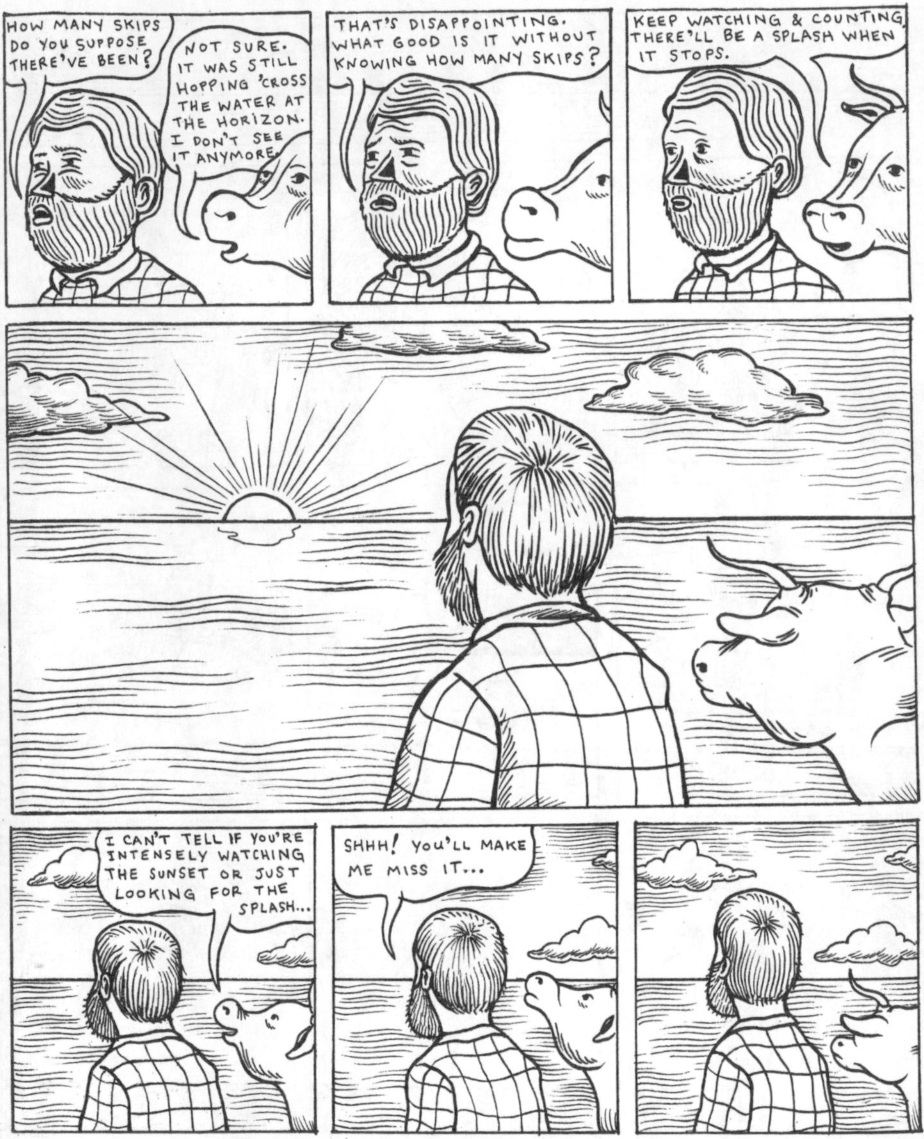
HOW MANY SKIPS DO YOU SUPPOSE THERE'VE BEEN?
NOT SURE. IT WAS STILL HOPPING 'CROSS THE WATER AT THE HORIZON. I DON'T SEE IT ANYMORE.
THAT'S DISAPPOINTING. WHAT GOOD IS IT WITHOUT KNOWING HOW MANY SKIPS?
KEEP WATCHING & COUNTING, THERE'LL BE A SPLASH WHEN IT STOPS.
I CAN'T TELL IF YOU'RE INTENSELY WATCHING THE SUNSET OR JUST LOOKING FOR THE SPLASH...
SHHH! YOU'LL MAKE ME MISS IT...

AN OCEAN IS BORN

Featuring Paul Bunyan

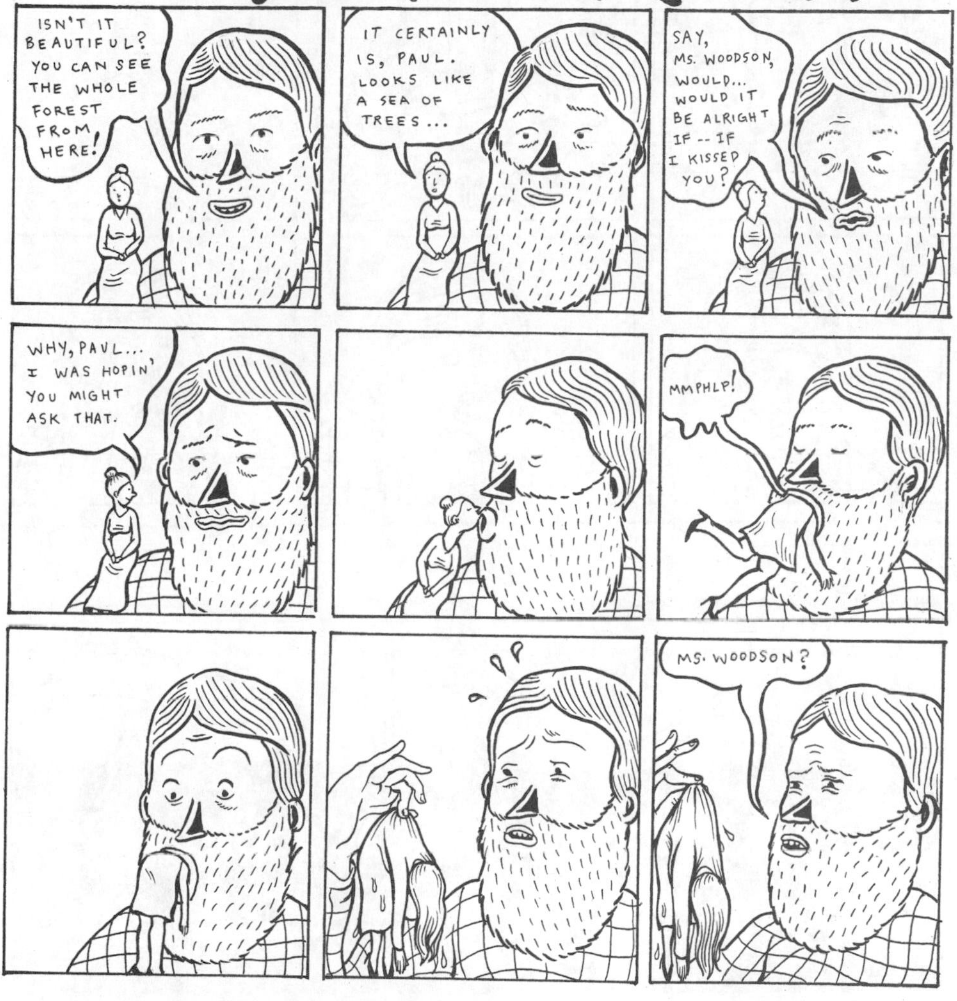

ISN'T IT BEAUTIFUL? YOU CAN SEE THE WHOLE FOREST FROM HERE!
IT CERTAINLY IS, PAUL. LOOKS LIKE A SEA OF TREES...
SAY, MS. WOODSON, WOULD... WOULD IT BE ALRIGHT IF -- IF I KISSED YOU?
WHY, PAUL... I WAS HOPIN' YOU MIGHT ASK THAT.
MMPHLP!
MS. WOODSON?

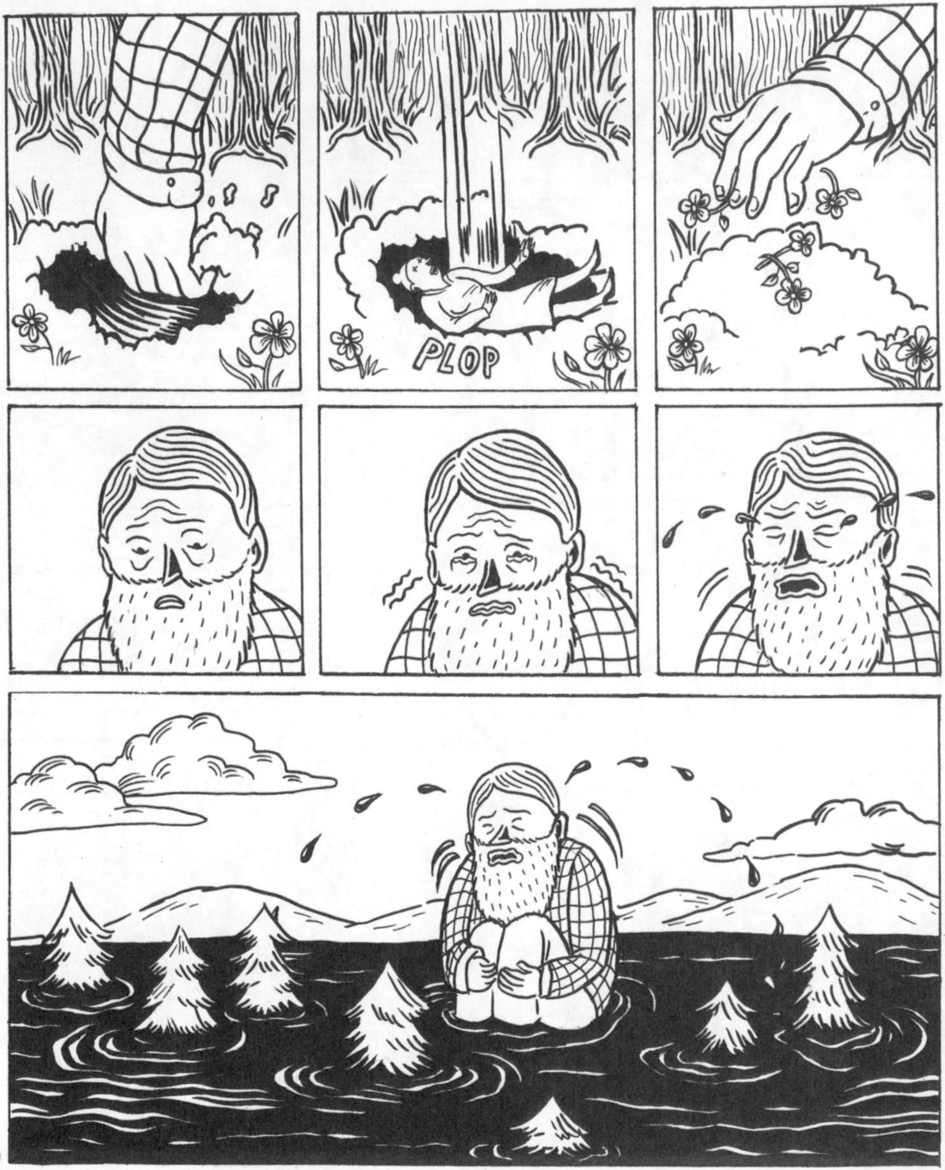
PLOP

WOODSMAN PETE IN THE CATCH

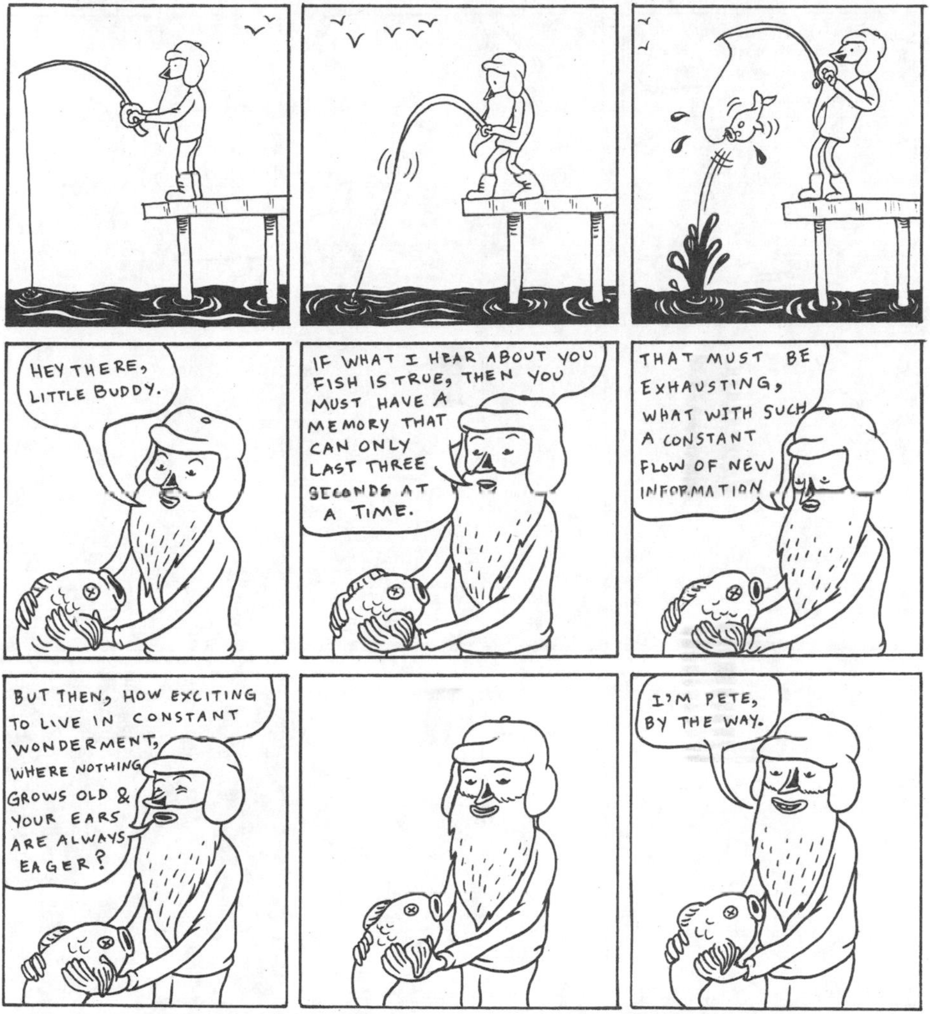
HEY THERE, LITTLE BUDDY.
IF WHAT I HEAR ABOUT YOU FISH IS TRUE, THEN YOU MUST HAVE A MEMORY THAT CAN ONLY LAST THREE SECONDS AT A TIME.
THAT MUST BE EXHAUSTING, WHAT WITH SUCH A CONSTANT FLOW OF NEW INFORMATION
BUT THEN, HOW EXCITING TO LIVE IN CONSTANT WONDERMENT, WHERE NOTHING GROWS OLD & YOUR EARS ARE ALWAYS EAGER?
I'M PETE, BY THE WAY.

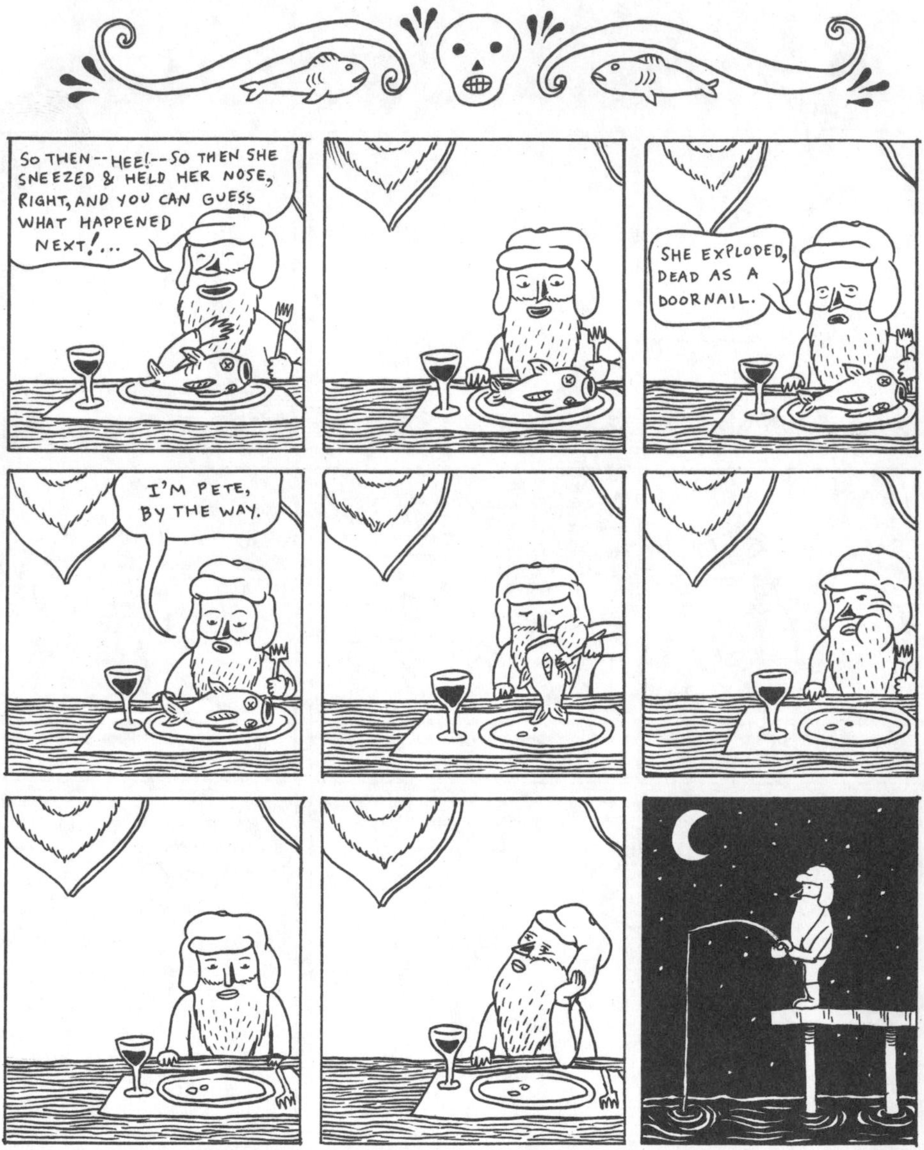
SO THEN--HEE!--SO THEN SHE SNEEZED & HELD HER NOSE, RIGHT, AND YOU CAN GUESS WHAT HAPPENED NEXT!...
SHE EXPLODED, DEAD AS A DOORNAIL.
I'M PETE, BY THE WAY.

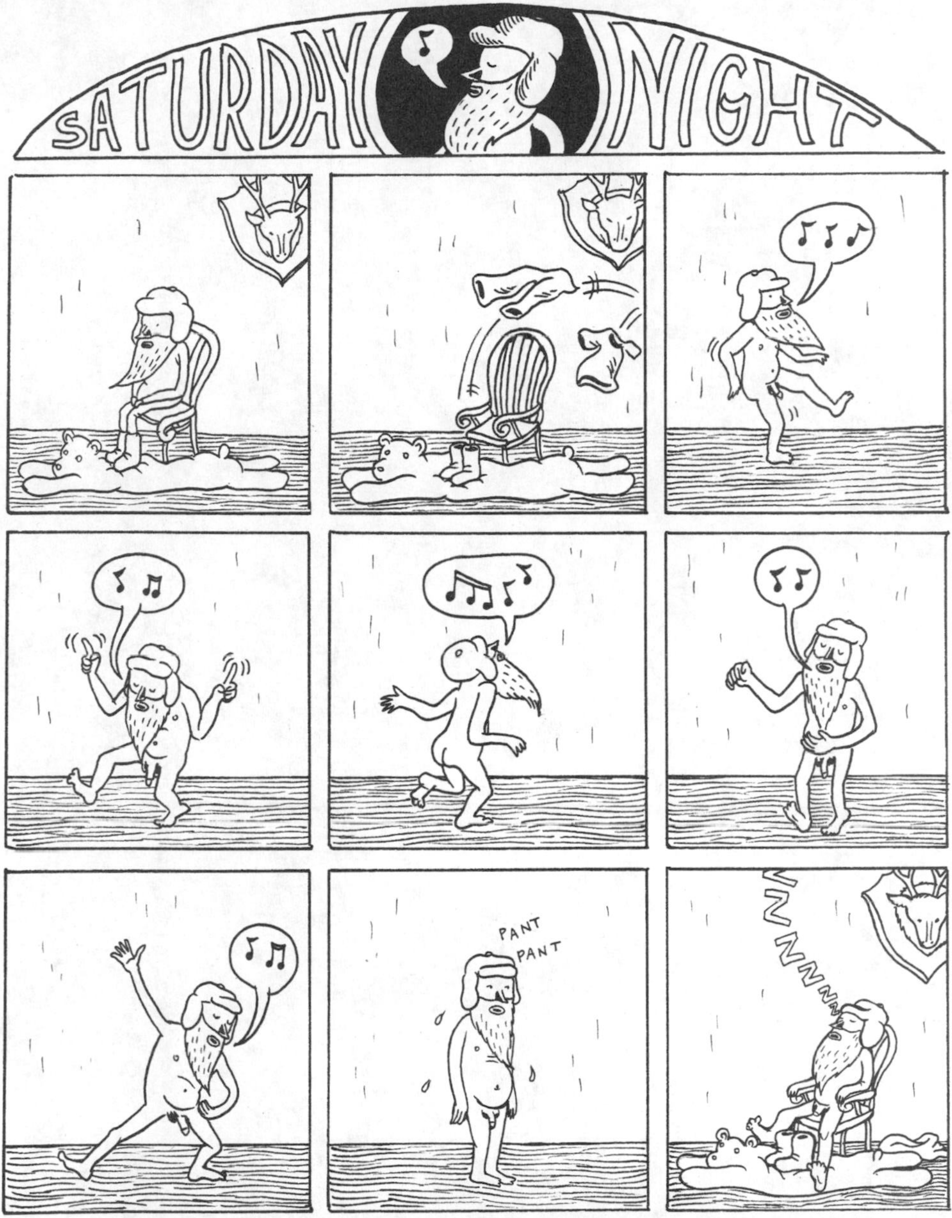
SATURDAY NIGHT
PANT
PANT

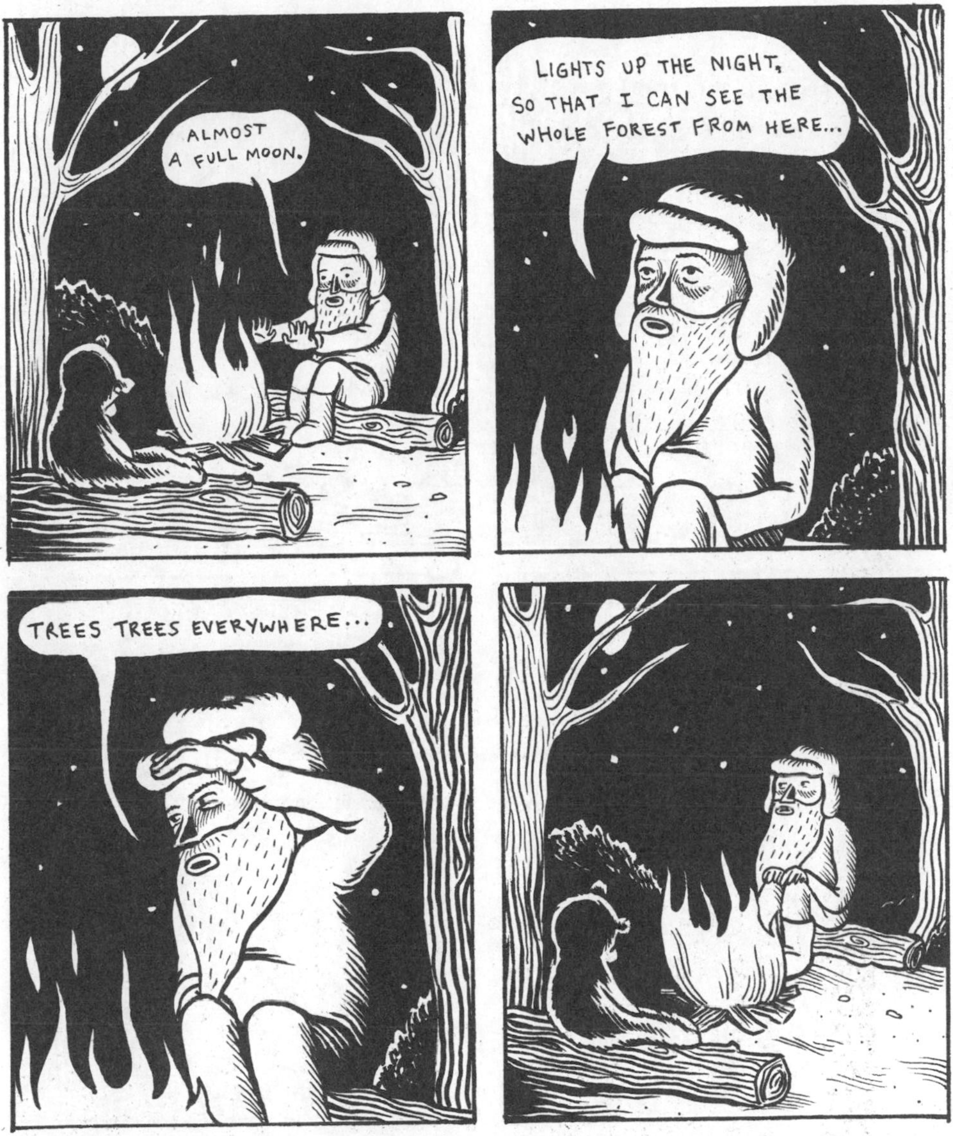
ALMOST A FULL MOON.
LIGHTS UP THE NIGHT, SO THAT I CAN SEE THE WHOLE FOREST FROM HERE...
TREES TREES EVERYWHERE...

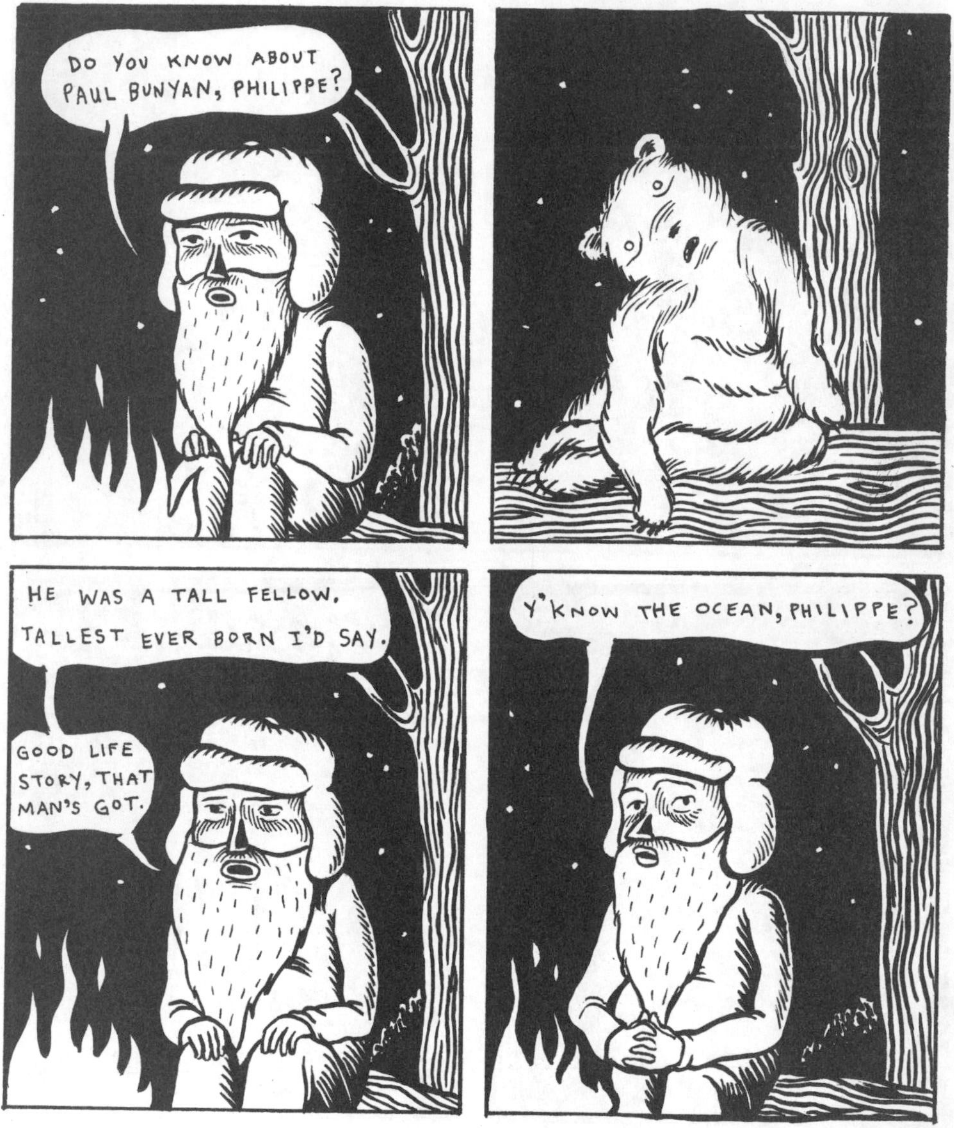
DO YOU KNOW ABOUT PAUL BUNYAN, PHILIPPE?
HE WAS A TALL FELLOW. TALLEST EVER BORN I'D SAY.
GOOD LIFE STORY, THAT MAN'S GOT.
Y'KNOW THE OCEAN, PHILIPPE?

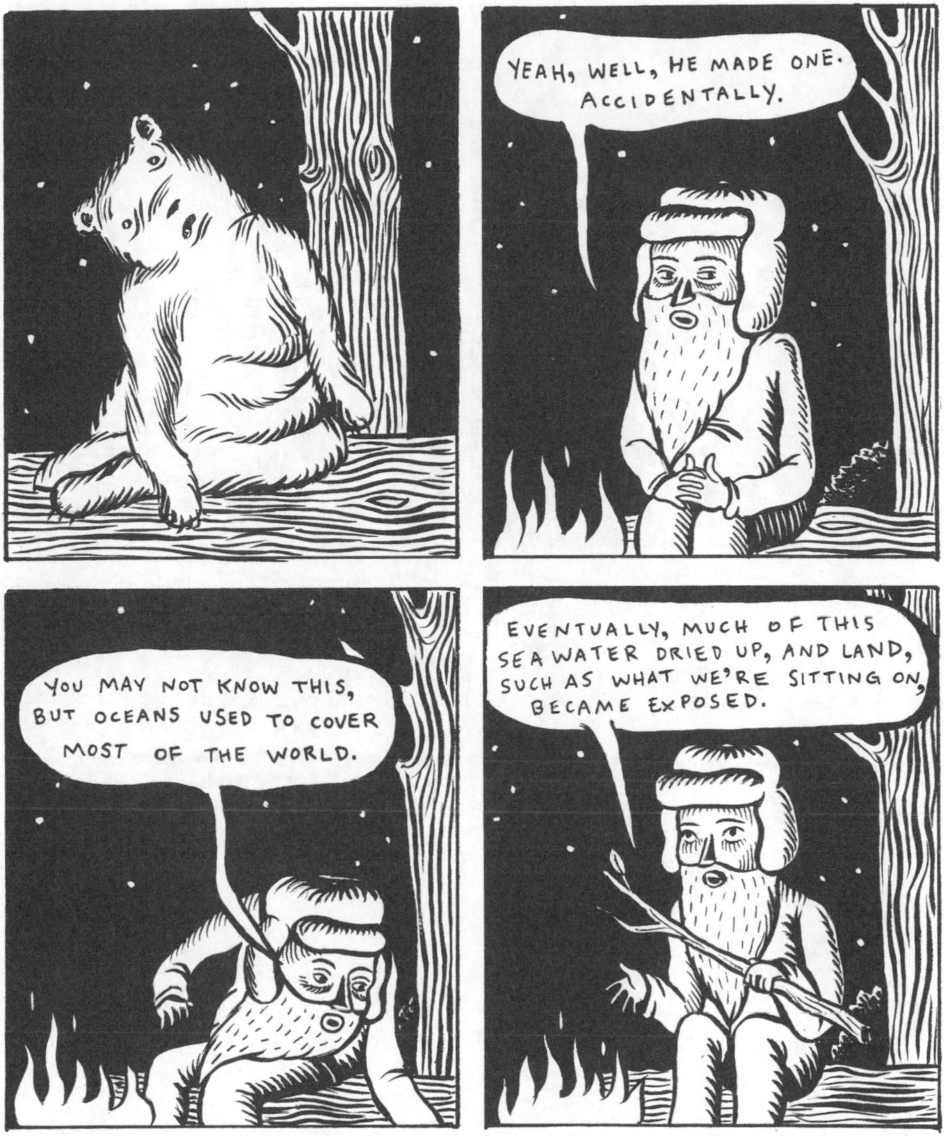
YEAH, WELL, HE MADE ONE. ACCIDENTALLY.
YOU MAY NOT KNOW THIS, BUT OCEANS USED TO COVER MOST OF THE WORLD.
EVENTUALLY, MUCH OF THIS SEAWATER DRIED UP, AND LAND, SUCH AS WHAT WE'RE SITTING ON, BECAME EXPOSED.

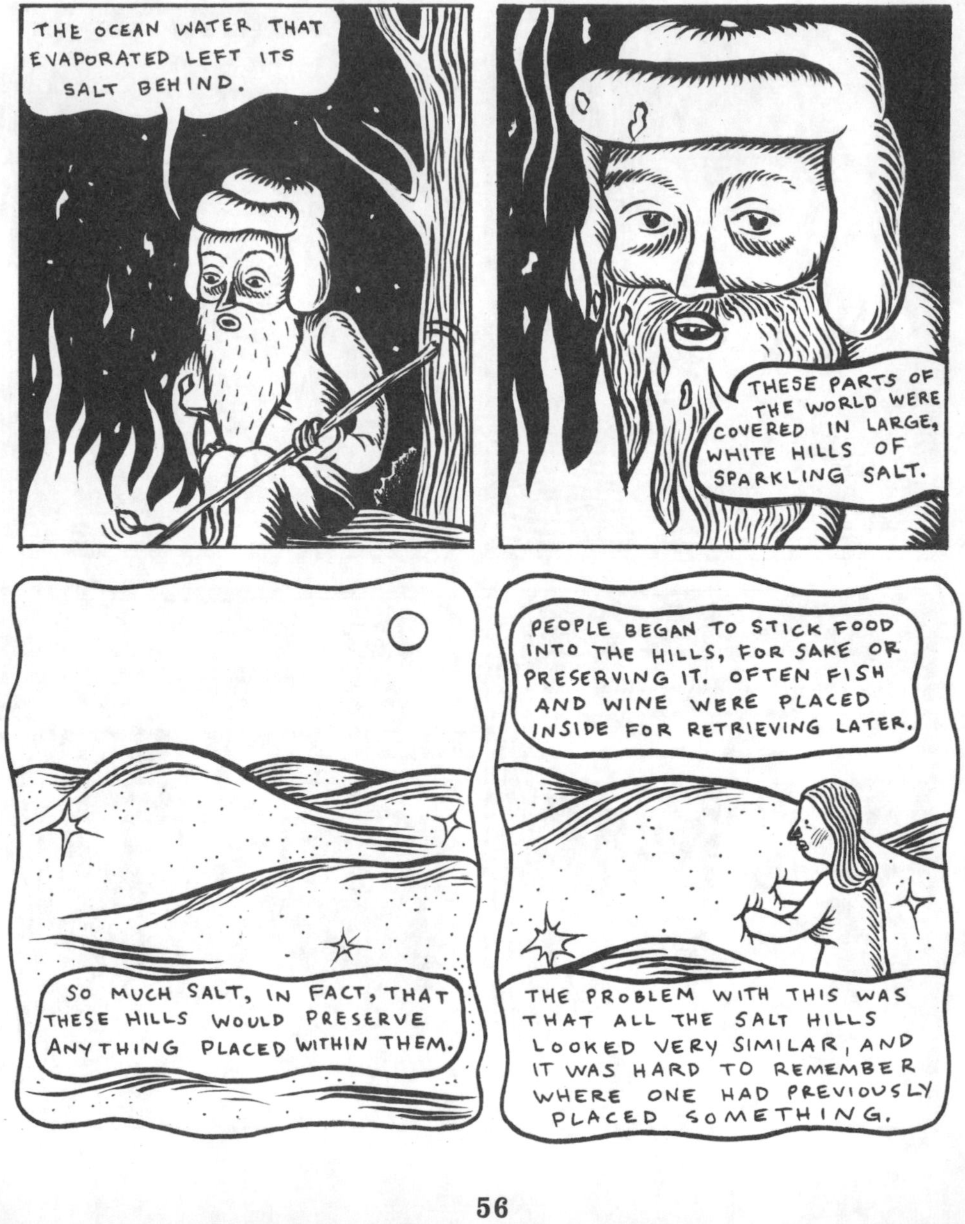
THE OCEAN WATER THAT EVAPORATED LEFT ITS SALT BEHIND.
THESE PARTS OF THE WORLD WERE COVERED IN LARGE, WHITE HILLS OF SPARKLING SALT.
SO MUCH SALT, IN FACT, THAT THESE HILLS WOULD PRESERVE ANYTHING PLACED WITHIN THEM.
PEOPLE BEGAN TO STICK FOOD INTO THE HILLS, FOR SAKE OR PRESERVING IT. OFTEN FISH AND WINE WERE PLACED INSIDE FOR RETRIEVING LATER.
THE PROBLEM WITH THIS WAS THAT ALL THE SALT HILLS LOOKED VERY SIMILAR, AND IT WAS HARD TO REMEMBER WHERE ONE HAD PREVIOUSLY PLACED SOMETHING.

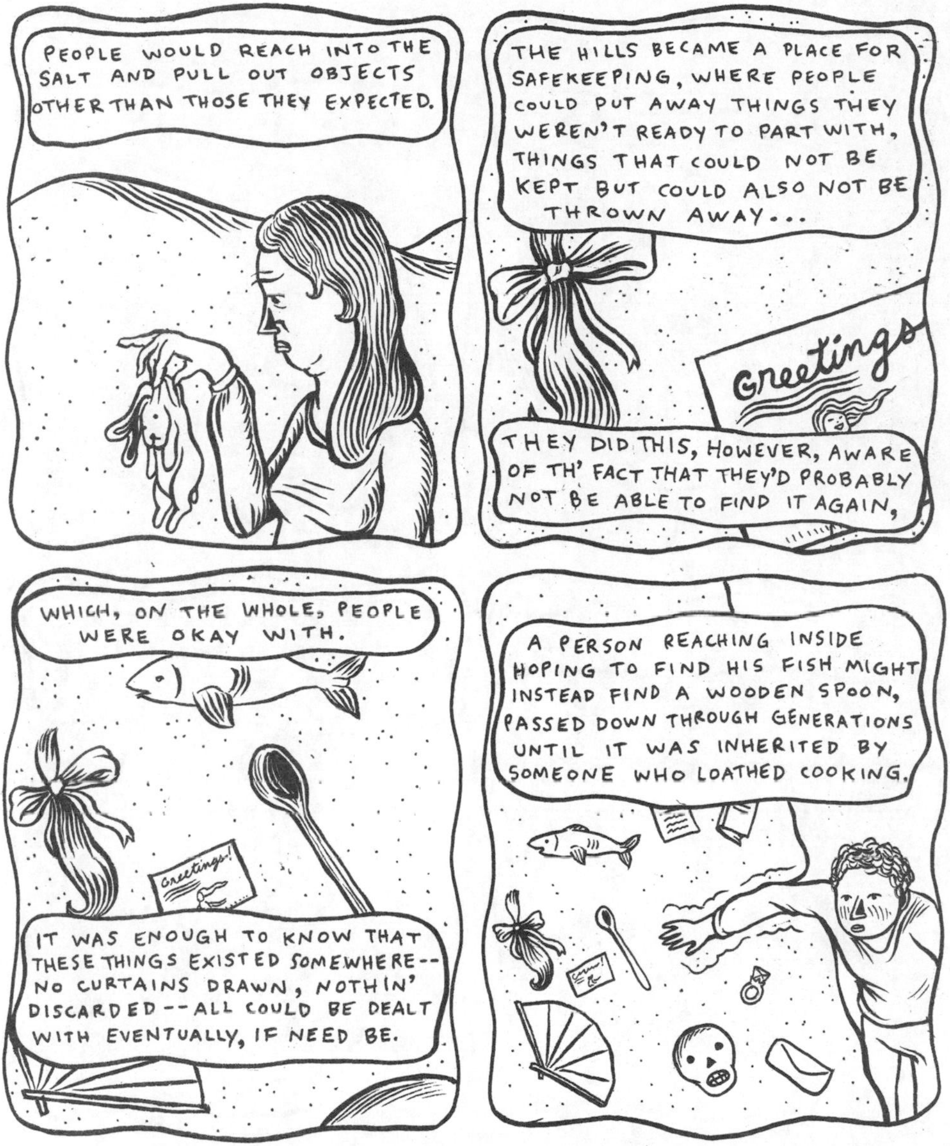
PEOPLE WOULD REACH INTO THE SALT AND PULL OUT OBJECTS OTHER THAN THOSE THEY EXPECTED.
THE HILLS BECAME A PLACE FOR SAFEKEEPING, WHERE PEOPLE COULD PUT AWAY THINGS THEY WEREN'T READY TO PART WITH, THINGS THAT COULD NOT BE KEPT BUT COULD ALSO NOT BE THROWN AWAY...
Greetings
THEY DID THIS, HOWEVER, AWARE OF TH' FACT THAT THEY'D PROBABLY NOT BE ABLE TO FIND IT AGAIN,
WHICH, ON THE WHOLE, PEOPLE WERE OKAY WITH.
Greetings!
IT WAS ENOUGH TO KNOW THAT THESE THINGS EXISTED SOMEWHERE-- NO CURTAINS DRAWN, NOTHIN' DISCARDED--ALL COULD BE DEALT WITH EVENTUALLY, IF NEED BE.
A PERSON REACHING INSIDE HOPING TO FIND HIS FISH MIGHT INSTEAD FIND A WOODEN SPOON, PASSED DOWN THROUGH GENERATIONS UNTIL IT WAS INHERITED BY SOMEONE WHO LOATHED COOKING.

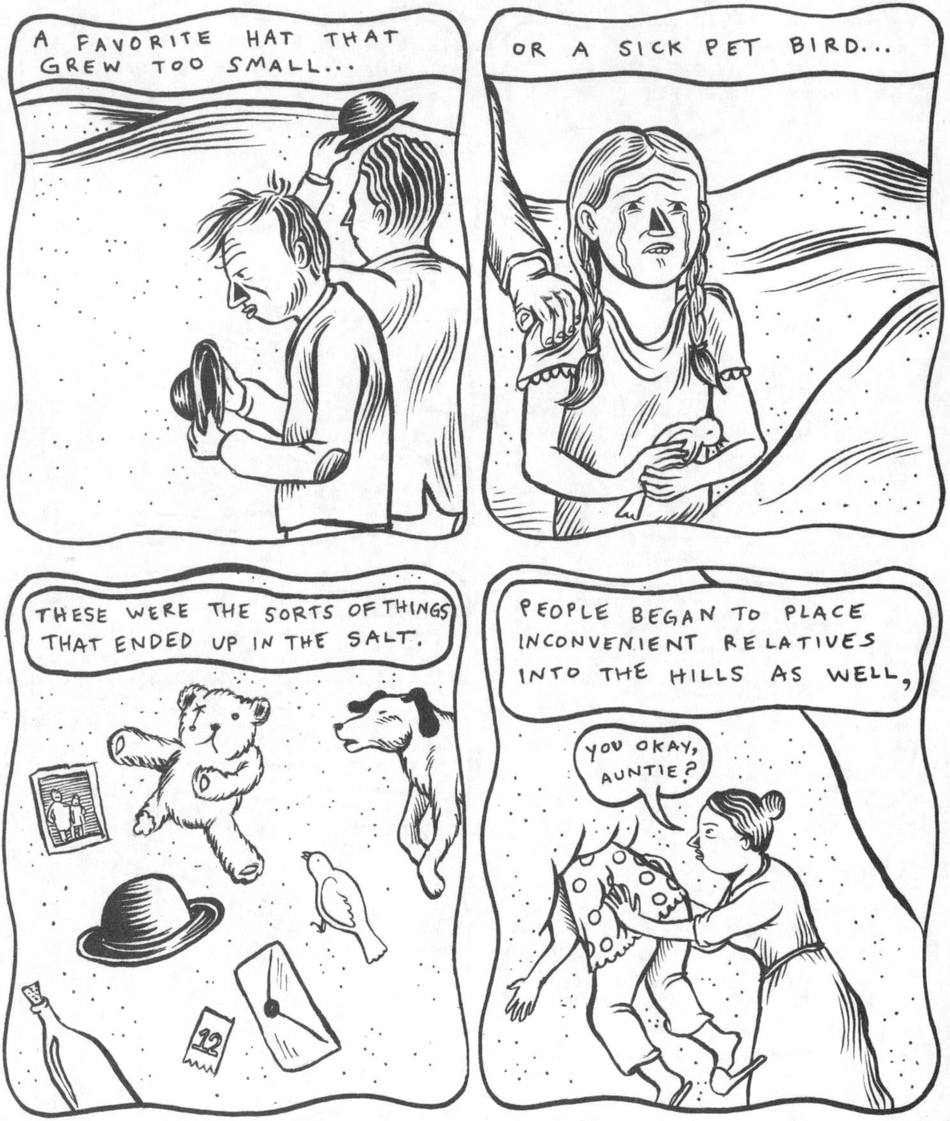
A FAVORITE HAT THAT GREW TOO SMALL...
OR A SICK PET BIRD...
THESE WERE THE SORTS OF THINGS THAT ENDED UP IN THE SALT.
12
PEOPLE BEGAN TO PLACE INCONVENIENT RELATIVES INTO THE HILLS AS WELL,
YOU OKAY, AUNTIE?

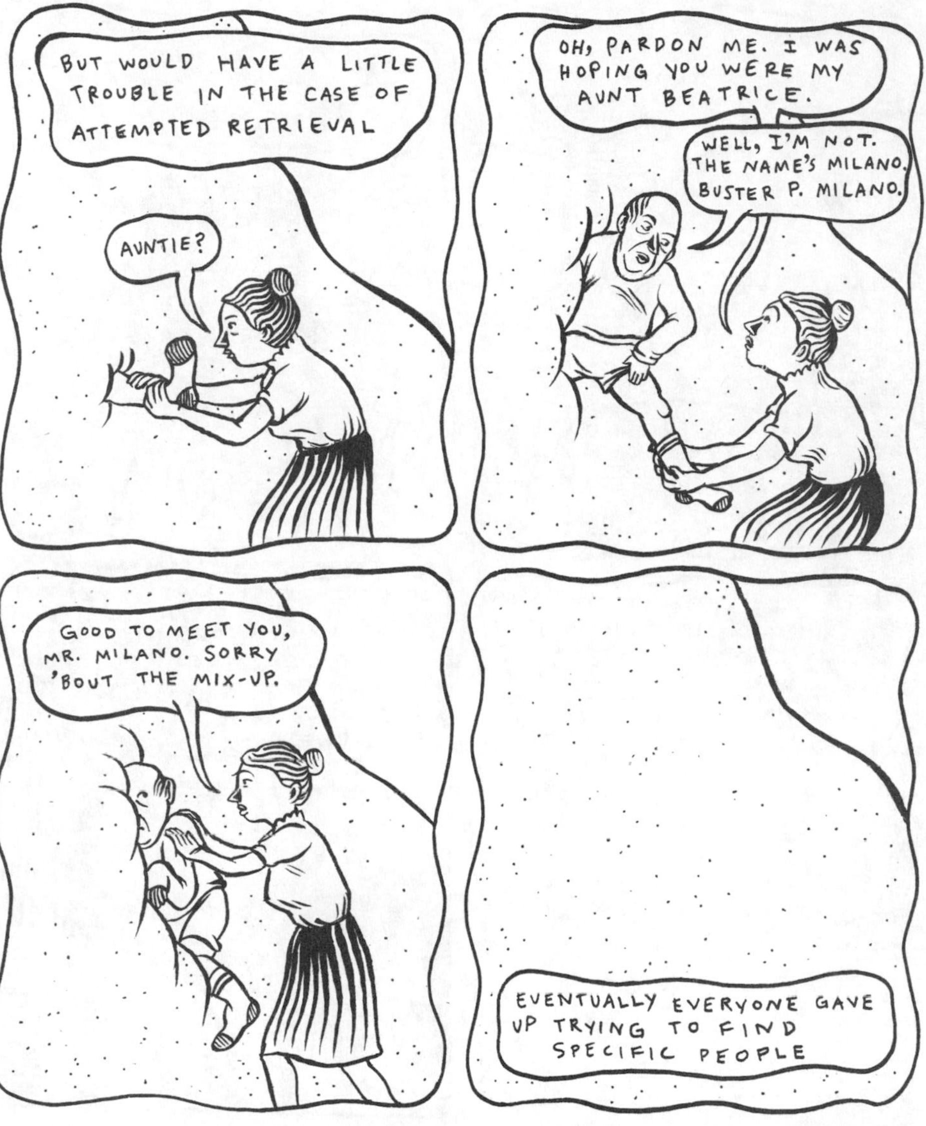
BUT WOULD HAVE A LITTLE TROUBLE IN THE CASE OF ATTEMPTED RETRIEVAL
AUNTIE?
OH, PARDON ME. I WAS HOPING YOU WERE MY AUNT BEATRICE.
WELL, I'M NOT. THE NAME'S MILANO. BUSTER P. MILANO.
GOOD TO MEET YOU, MR. MILANO. SORRY 'BOUT THE MIX-UP.
EVENTUALLY EVERYONE GAVE UP TRYING TO FIND SPECIFIC PEOPLE

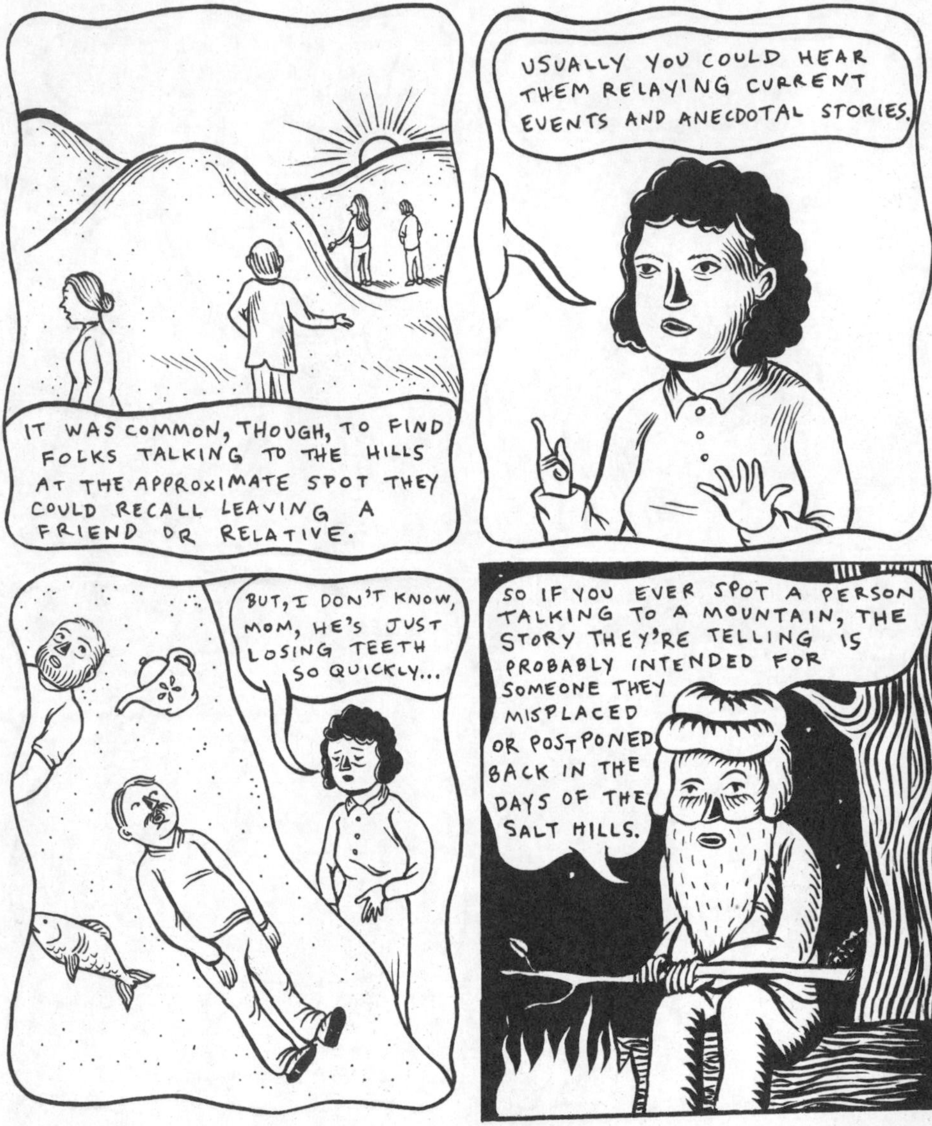
IT WAS COMMON, THOUGH, TO FIND FOLKS TALKING TO THE HILLS AT THE APPROXIMATE SPOT THEY COULD RECALL LEAVING A FRIEND OR RELATIVE.
USUALLY YOU COULD HEAR THEM RELAYING CURRENT EVENTS AND ANECDOTAL STORIES.
BUT, I DON'T KNOW, MOM, HE'S JUST LOSING TEETH SO QUICKLY...
SO IF YOU EVER SPOT A PERSON TALKING TO A MOUNTAIN, THE STORY THEY'RE TELLING IS PROBABLY INTENDED FOR SOMEONE THEY MISPLACED OR POSTPONED BACK IN THE DAYS OF THE SALT HILLS.

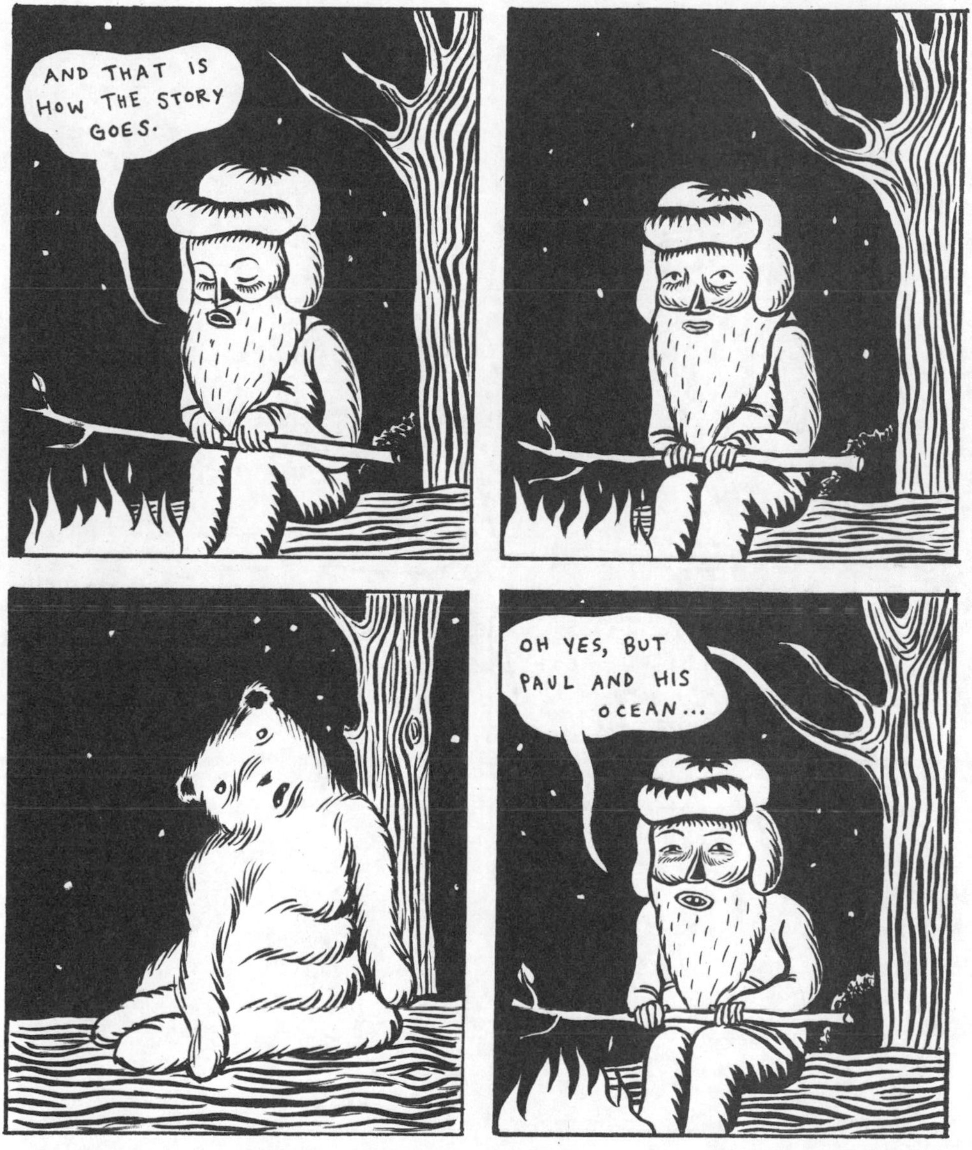
AND THAT IS HOW THE STORY GOES.
OH YES, BUT PAUL AND HIS OCEAN...

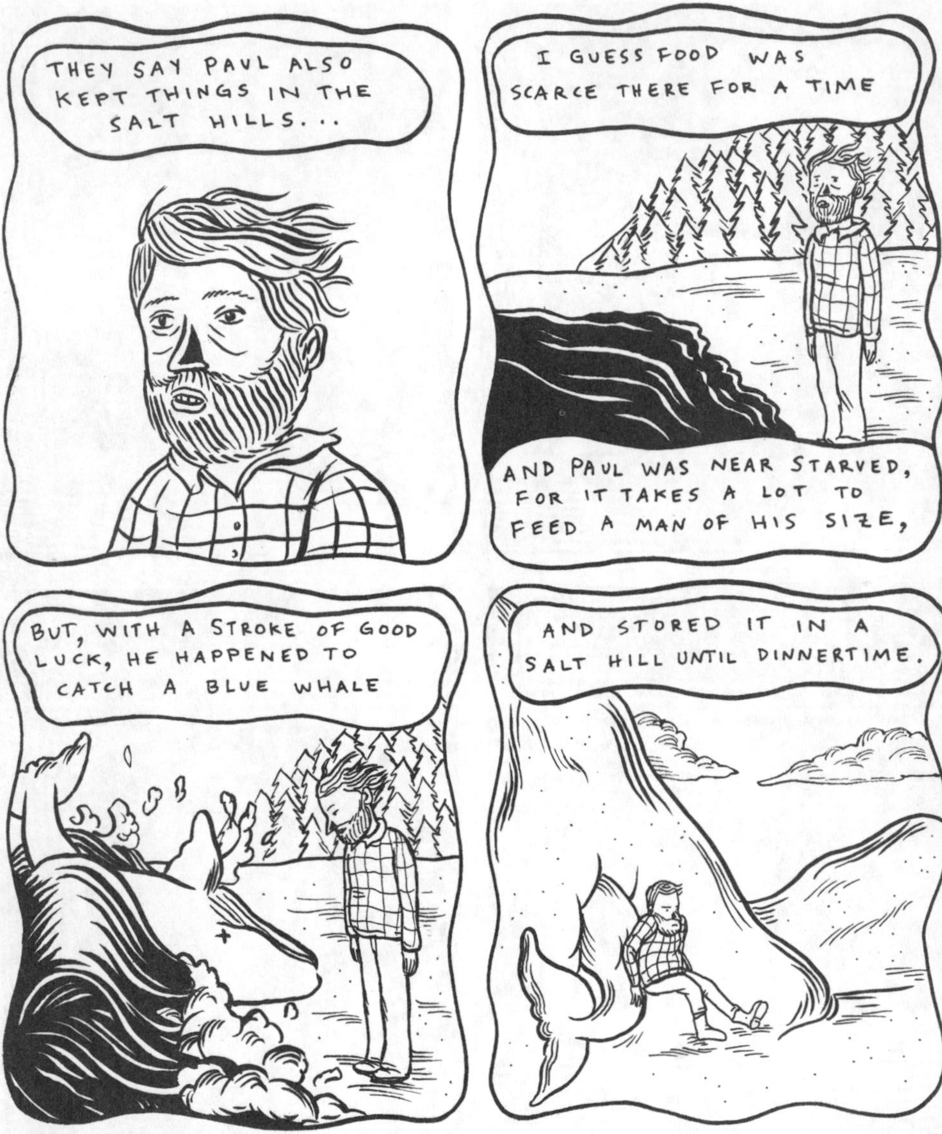
THEY SAY PAUL ALSO KEPT THINGS IN THE SALT HILLS...
I GUESS FOOD WAS SCARCE THERE FOR A TIME
AND PAUL WAS NEAR STARVED, FOR IT TAKES A LOT TO FEED A MAN OF HIS SIZE,
BUT, WITH A STROKE OF GOOD LUCK, HE HAPPENED TO CATCH A BLUE WHALE
AND STORED IT IN A SALT HILL UNTIL DINNERTIME.

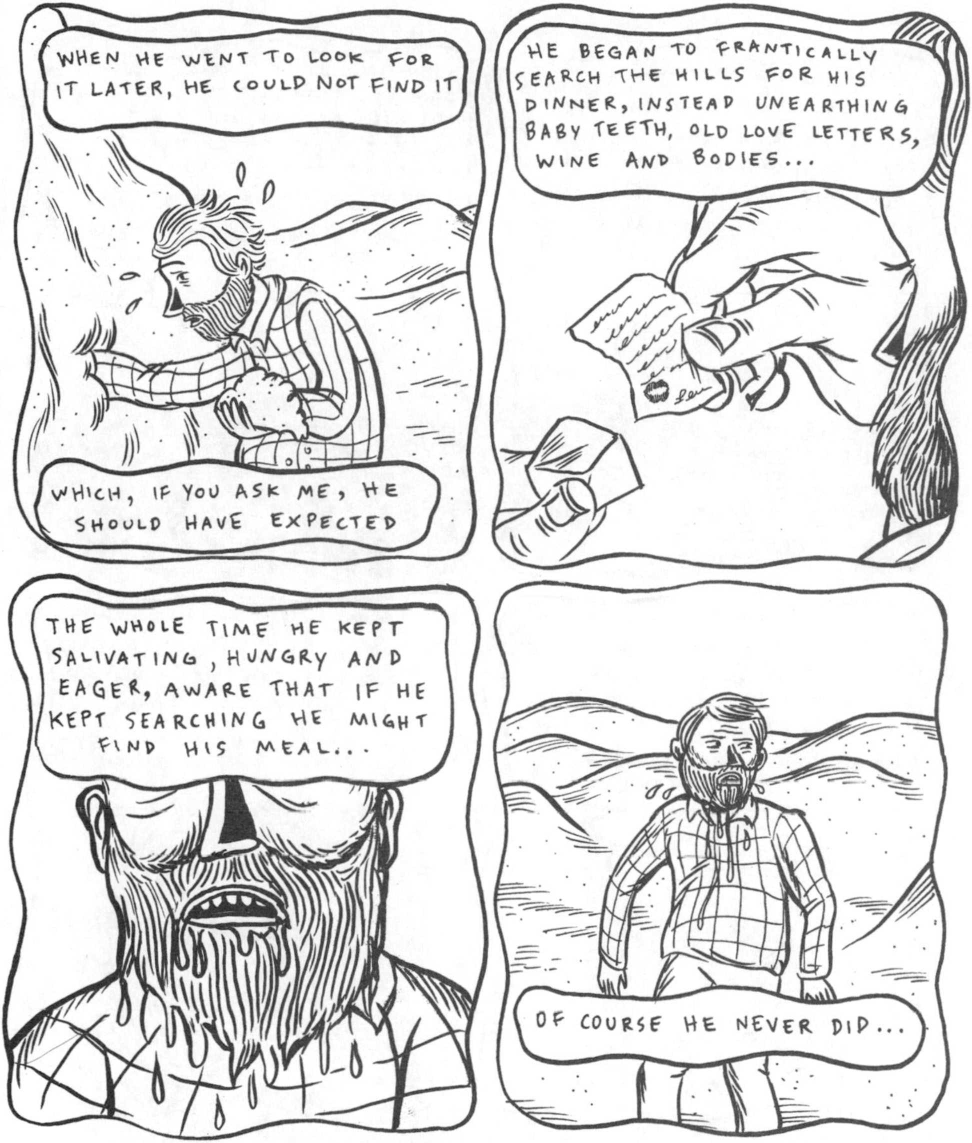
WHEN HE WENT TO LOOK FOR IT LATER, HE COULD NOT FIND IT
WHICH, IF YOU ASK ME, HE SHOULD HAVE EXPECTED
HE BEGAN TO FRANTICALLY SEARCH THE HILLS FOR HIS DINNER, INSTEAD UNEARTHING BABY TEETH, OLD LOVE LETTERS, WINE AND BODIES...
THE WHOLE TIME HE KEPT SALIVATING, HUNGRY AND EAGER, AWARE THAT IF HE KEPT SEARCHING HE MIGHT FIND HIS MEAL...
OF COURSE HE NEVER DID...

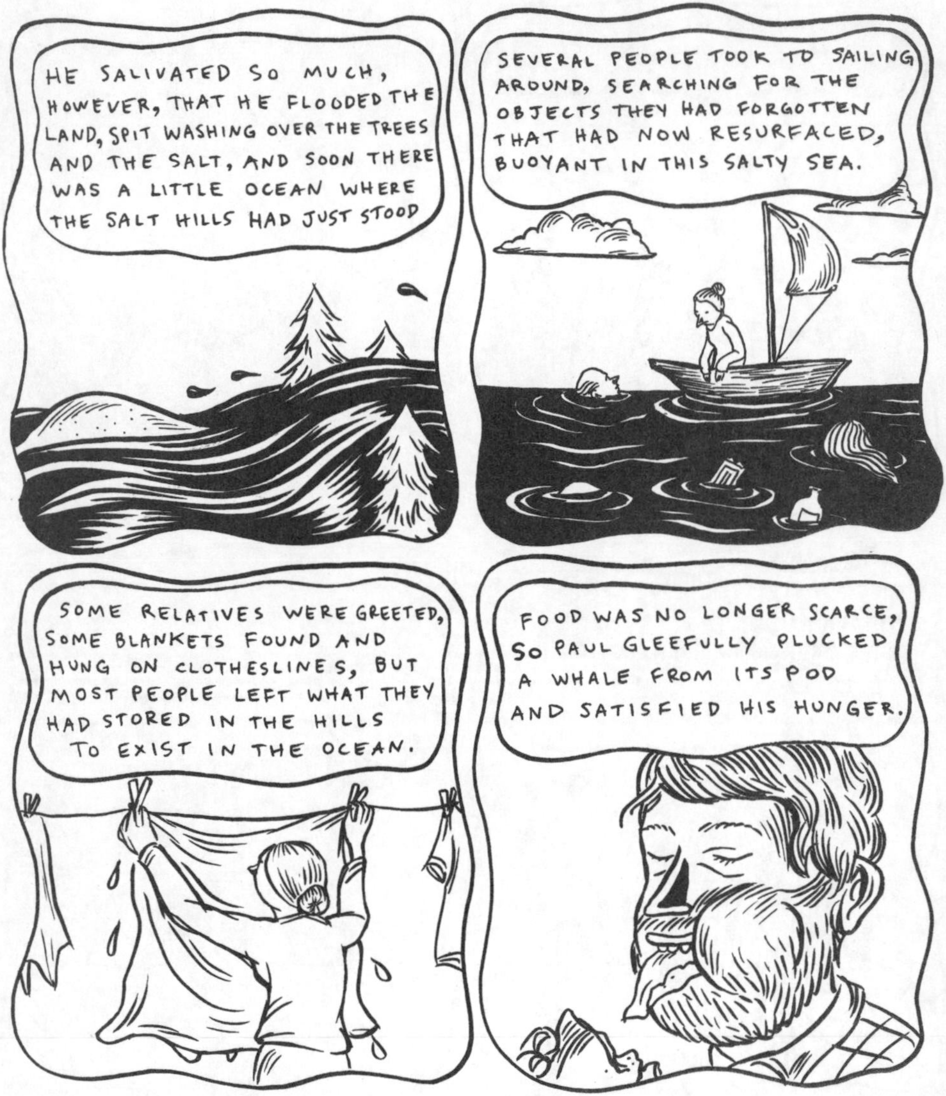
HE SALIVATED SO MUCH, HOWEVER, THAT HE FLOODED THE LAND, SPIT WASHING OVER THE TREES AND THE SALT, AND SOON THERE WAS A LITTLE OCEAN WHERE THE SALT HILLS HAD JUST STOOD
SEVERAL PEOPLE TOOK TO SAILING AROUND, SEARCHING FOR THE OBJECTS THEY HAD FORGOTTEN THAT HAD NOW RESURFACED, BUOYANT IN THIS SALTY SEA.
SOME RELATIVES WERE GREETED, SOME BLANKETS FOUND AND HUNG ON CLOTHESLINES, BUT MOST PEOPLE LEFT WHAT THEY HAD STORED IN THE HILLS TO EXIST IN THE OCEAN.
FOOD WAS NO LONGER SCARCE, SO PAUL GLEEFULLY PLUCKED A WHALE FROM ITS POD AND SATISFIED HIS HUNGER.

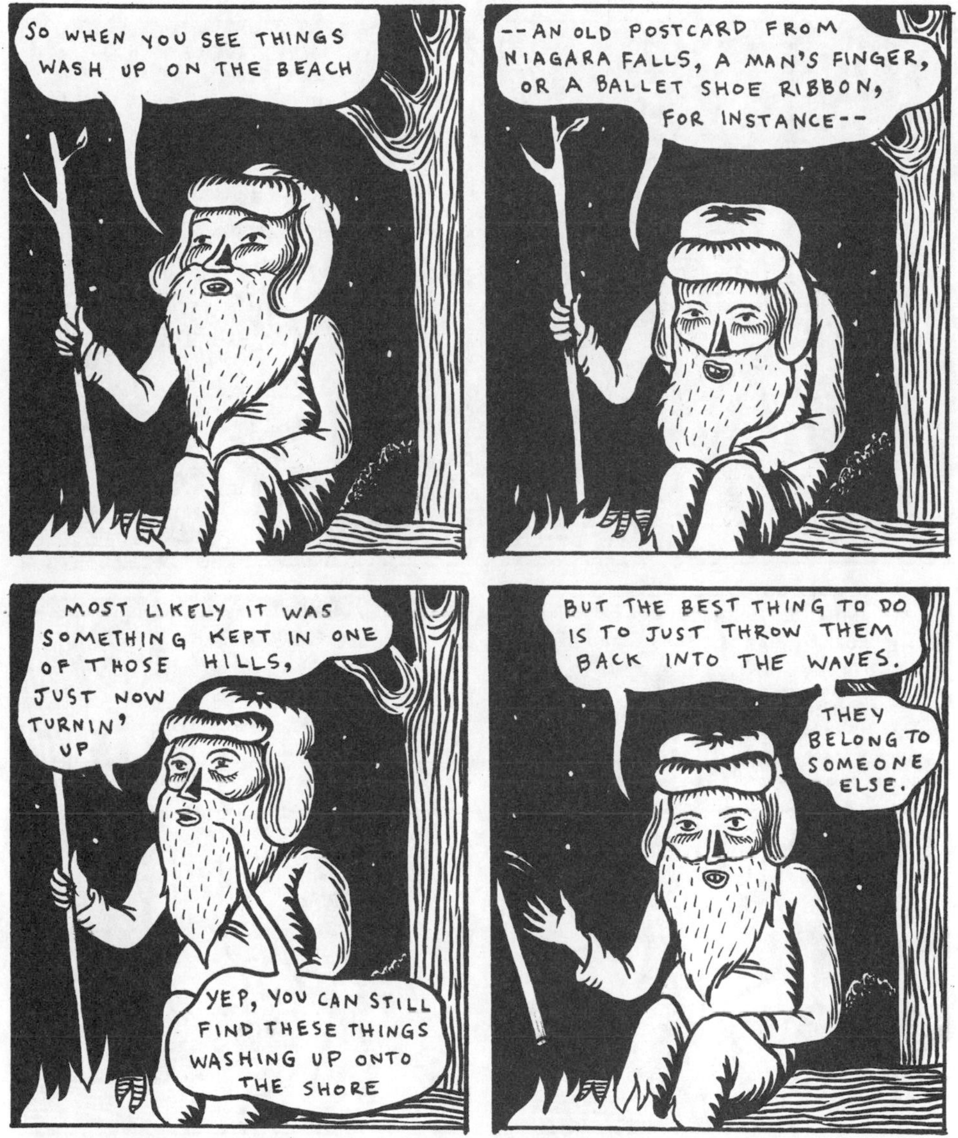

SO WHEN YOU SEE THINGS WASH UP ON THE BEACH
--AN OLD POSTCARD FROM NIAGARA FALLS, A MAN'S FINGER, OR A BALLET SHOE RIBBON, FOR INSTANCE--
MOST LIKELY IT WAS SOMETHING KEPT IN ONE OF THOSE HILLS,
JUST NOW TURNIN' UP
YEP, YOU CAN STILL FIND THESE THINGS WASHING UP ONTO THE SHORE
BUT THE BEST THING TO DO IS TO JUST THROW THEM BACK INTO THE WAVES.
THEY BELONG TO SOMEONE ELSE.

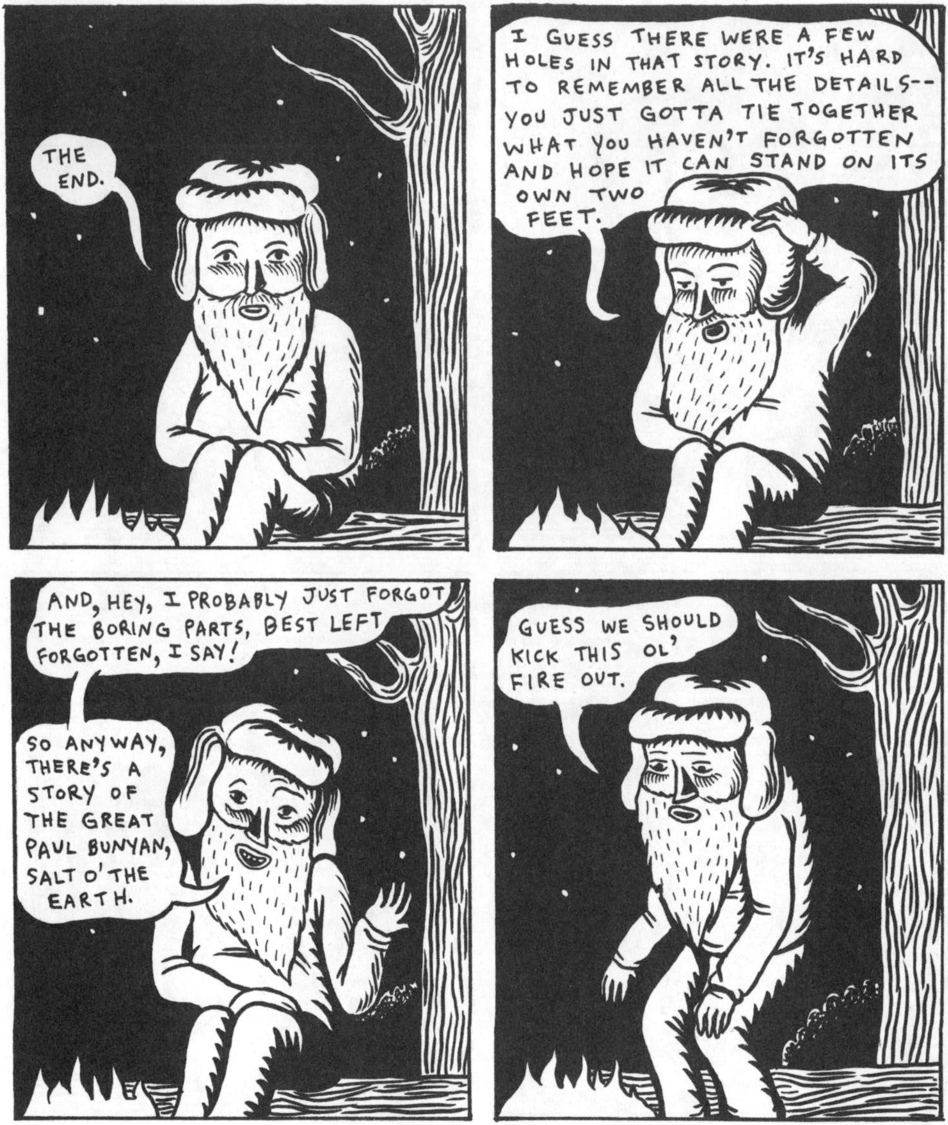
THE END.
I GUESS THERE WERE A FEW HOLES IN THAT STORY. IT'S HARD TO REMEMBER ALL THE DETAILS-- YOU JUST GOTTA TIE TOGETHER WHAT YOU HAVEN'T FORGOTTEN AND HOPE IT CAN STAND ON ITS OWN TWO FEET.
AND, HEY, I PROBABLY JUST FORGOT THE BORING PARTS, BEST LEFT FORGOTTEN, I SAY!
SO ANYWAY, THERE'S A STORY OF THE GREAT PAUL BUNYAN, SALT O' THE EARTH.
GUESS WE SHOULD KICK THIS OL' FIRE OUT.

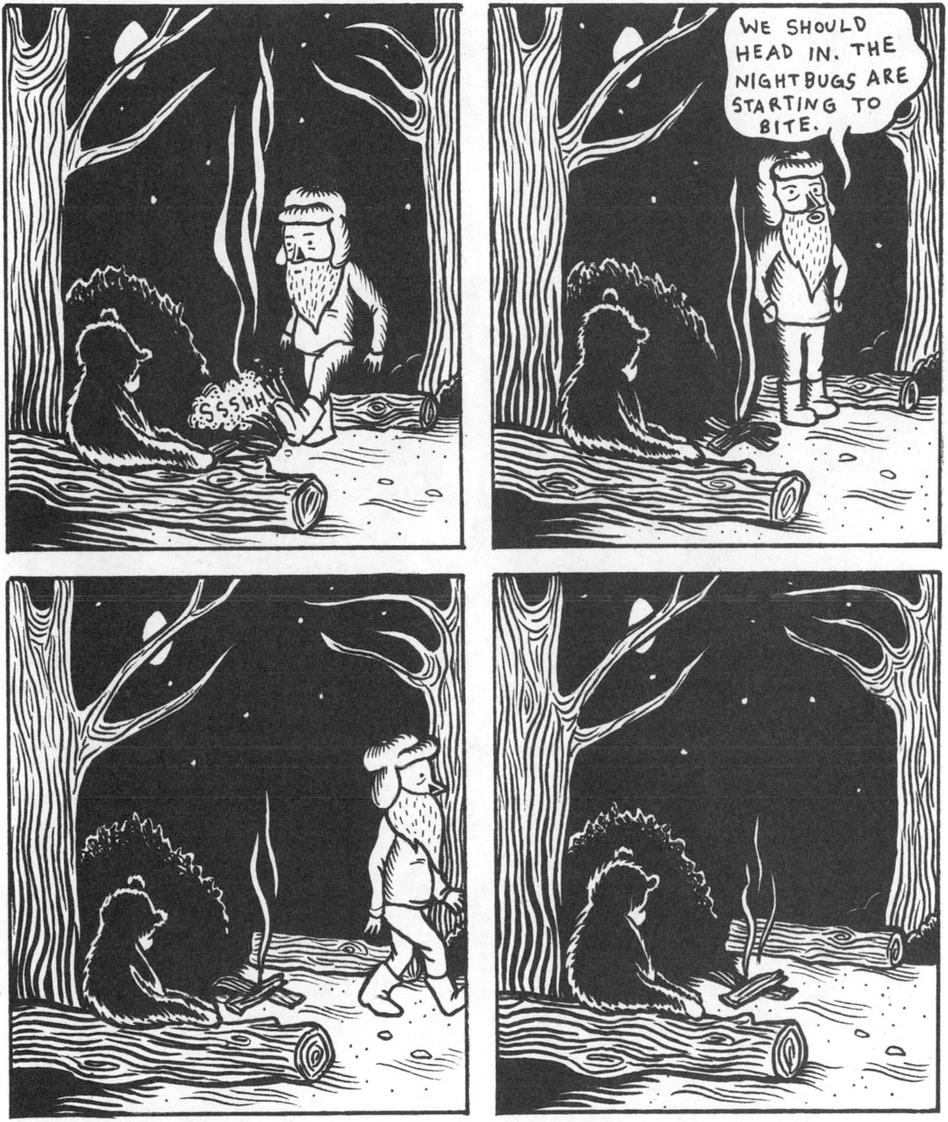
SSSHH
WE SHOULD HEAD IN. THE NIGHTBUGS ARE STARTING TO BITE.

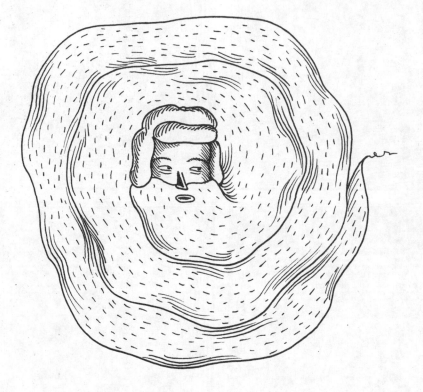

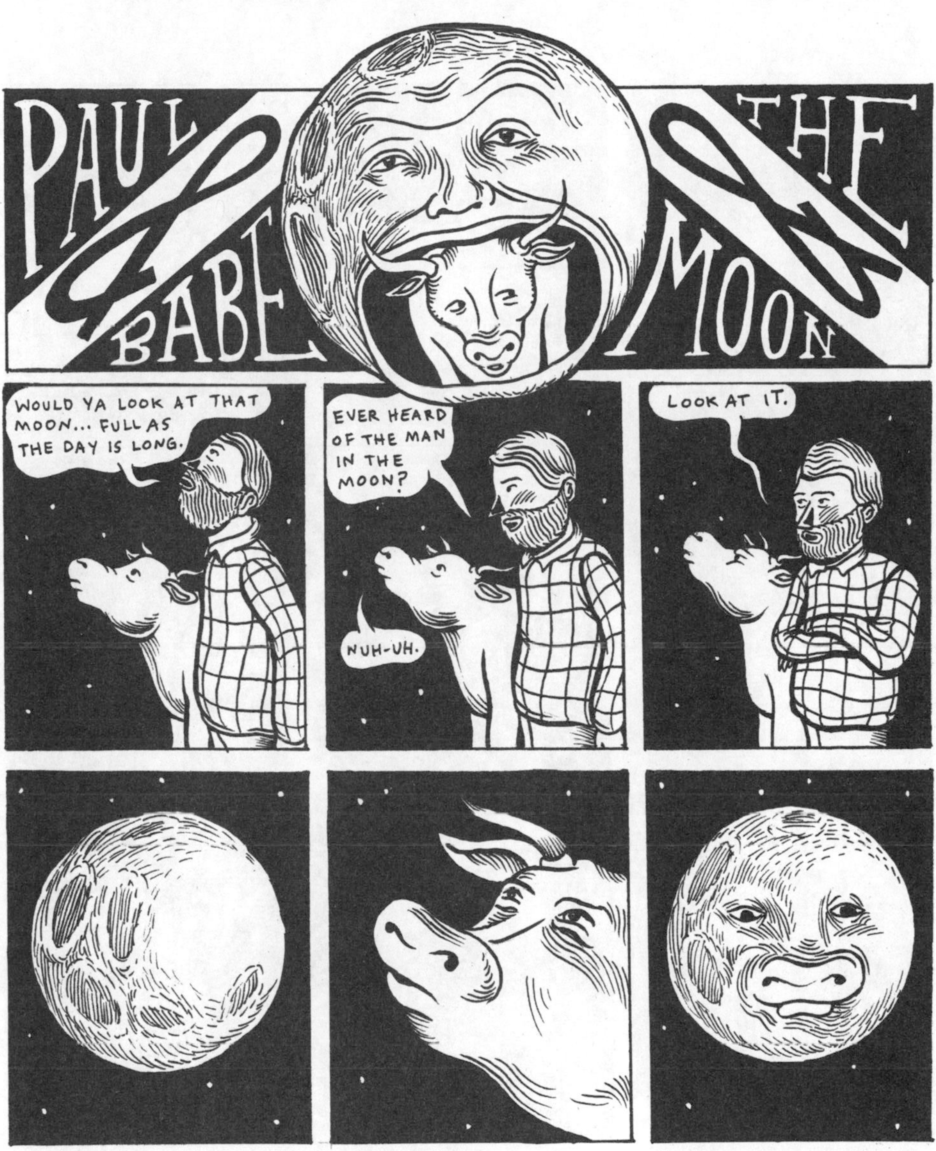
PAUL & BABE & THE MOON
WOULD YA LOOK AT THAT MOON... FULL AS THE DAY IS LONG.
EVER HEARD OF THE MAN IN THE MOON?
NUH-UH.
LOOK AT IT.

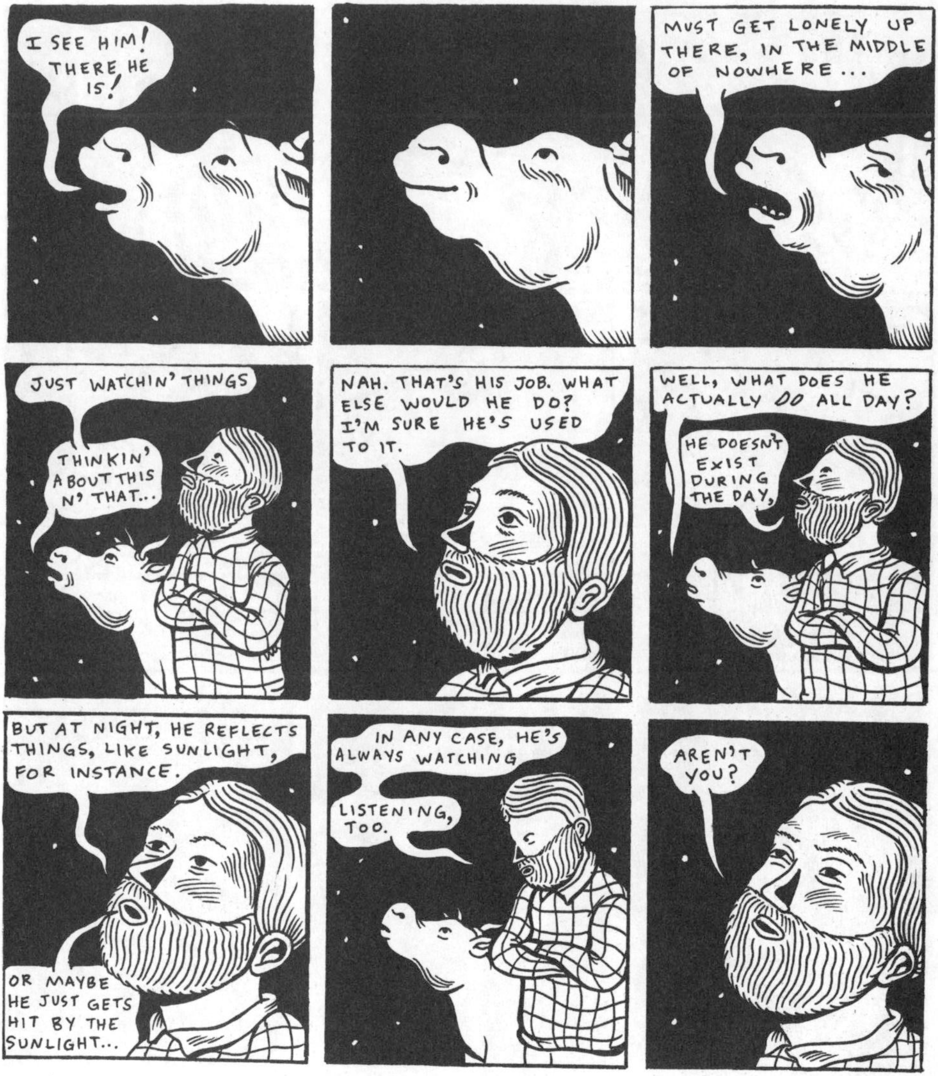
I SEE HIM! THERE HE IS!
MUST GET LONELY UP THERE, IN THE MIDDLE OF NOWHERE...
JUST WATCHIN' THINGS
THINKIN' ABOUT THIS N' THAT...
NAH. THAT'S HIS JOB. WHAT ELSE WOULD HE DO? I'M SURE HE'S USED TO IT.
WELL, WHAT DOES HE ACTUALLY DO ALL DAY?
HE DOESN'T EXIST DURING THE DAY,
BUT AT NIGHT, HE REFLECTS THINGS, LIKE SUNLIGHT, FOR INSTANCE.
OR MAYBE HE JUST GETS HIT BY THE SUNLIGHT...
IN ANY CASE, HE'S ALWAYS WATCHING
LISTENING, TOO.
AREN'T YOU?

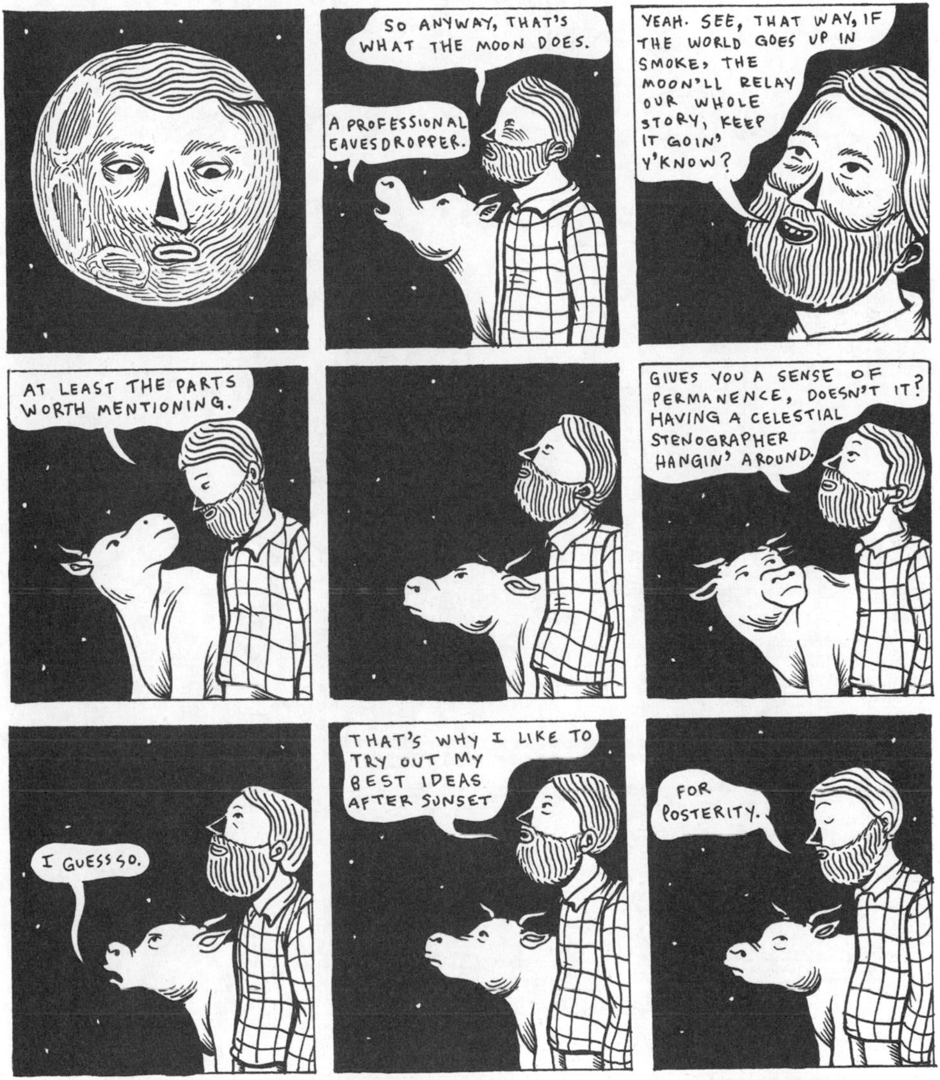
SO ANYWAY, THAT'S WHAT THE MOON DOES.
A PROFESSIONAL EAVESDROPPER.
YEAH. SEE, THAT WAY, IF THE WORLD GOES UP IN SMOKE, THE MOON'LL RELAY OUR WHOLE STORY, KEEP IT GOIN' Y'KNOW?
AT LEAST THE PARTS WORTH MENTIONING.
GIVES YOU A SENSE OF PERMANENCE, DOESN'T IT? HAVING A CELESTIAL STENOGRAPHER HANGIN' AROUND.
I GUESS SO.
THAT'S WHY I LIKE TO TRY OUT MY BEST IDEAS AFTER SUNSET
FOR POSTERITY.

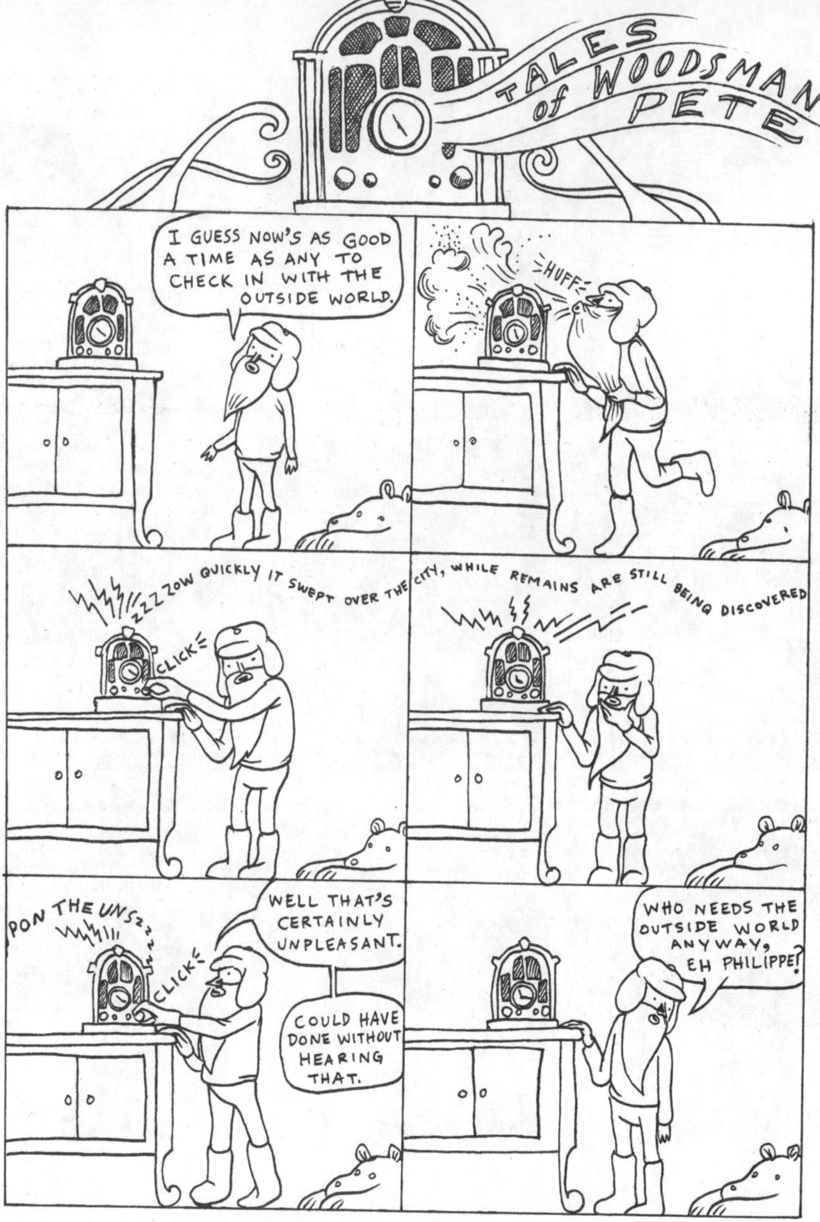
TALES of WOODSMAN PETE
I GUESS NOW'S AS GOOD A TIME AS ANY TO CHECK IN WITH THE OUTSIDE WORLD.
HUFF
ZZZZOW QUICKLY IT SWEPT OVER THE CITY, WHILE REMAINS ARE STILL BEING DISCOVERED
CLICK
PON THE UNSZZZZ
CLICK
WELL THAT'S CERTAINLY UNPLEASANT.
COULD HAVE DONE WITHOUT HEARING THAT.
WHO NEEDS THE OUTSIDE WORLD ANYWAY, EH PHILIPPE?

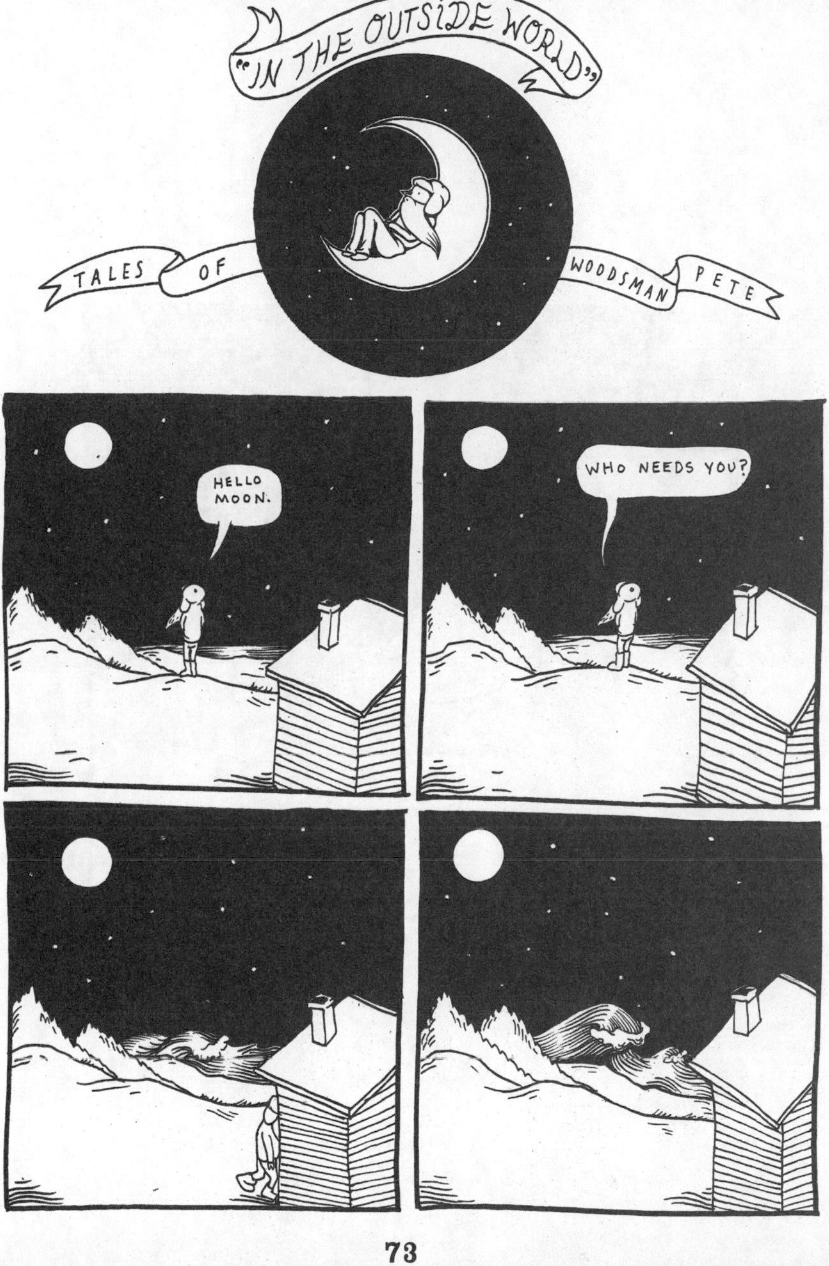
"IN THE OUTSIDE WORLD"
TALES OF WOODSMAN PETE
HELLO MOON.
WHO NEEDS YOU?

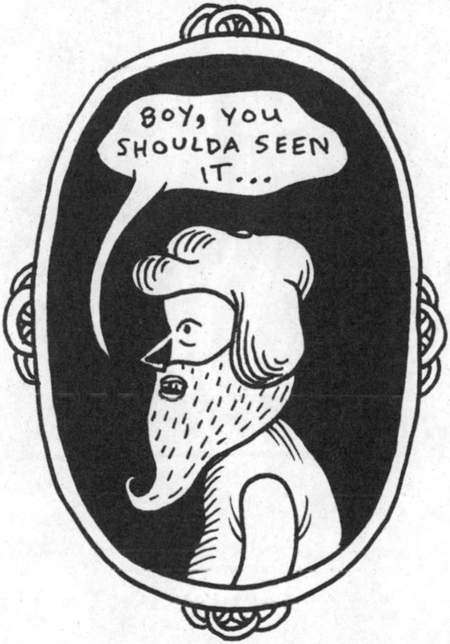
BOY, YOU SHOULDA SEEN IT...

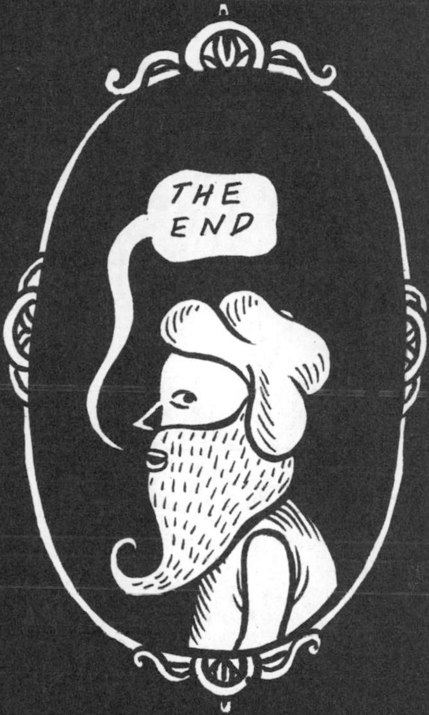
THE END

Thanks

Lilli Carré was born in 1983 in Los Angeles. She currently lives in Chicago, and still looks at snow with disbelief.

Thanks to Chris Sullivan, Marco Torres, Paul Hornschemeier, Alexander Stewart, Jessica Abel, Matt Madden, Chris & Brett at Top Shelf, Perrin Iacopino, Ivan Mairesse, Mark "that's a whole 'nother kettle of fish" Booth, Chelsea Wagner, the folks from the comic book stores of Chicago, and Lynda & Claire Carré.